WEST CHARLESTON LIBRARY

D0397009

7/13/44 ④ 9/22/44

LAS VEGAS · CLARK COUNTY.
LIBRARY DISTRICT
833 LAS VEGAS BLVD. N.
LAS VEGAS, NEVADA 89101

The Other Side of Death

Books by J. Sidlow Baxter

Awake, My Heart
Does God Still Guide?
Explore the Book
The God You Should Know
Mark These Men
The Other Side of Death
The Strategic Grasp of the Bible

The Christian Sanctification Series

Our High Calling
A New Call to Holiness
His Deeper Work in Us

The Other Side of Death

What the Bible Teaches About Heaven and Hell

J. Sidlow Baxter

kregel
PUBLICATIONS

Grand Rapids, MI 49501

The Other Side of Death

Copyright © 1987 by J. Sidlow Baxter

Published in 1997 by Kregel Publications, a division of Kregel, Inc., P.O. Box 2607, Grand Rapids, MI 49501. Kregel Publications provides trusted, biblical publications for Christian growth and service. Your comments and suggestions are valued.

All rights reserved. No part of this book may be reproduced, stored in a retrieval system, or transmitted in any form or by any means—electronic, mechanical, photocopy, recording, or otherwise—without written permission of the publisher, except for brief quotations in printed reviews.

Unless otherwise noted, all Scripture is from the English Revised Version of the King James Version of the Bible. Some words and phrases are the author's own traslation.

For more information about Kregel Publications, visit our web site at http://www.kregel.com.

Cover design: Alan G. Hartman

Library of Congress Cataloging-in-Publication Data
Baxter, J. Sidlow (James Sidlow).
   The other side of death / J. Sidlow Baxter.
       p.   cm.
Originally published: Wheaton, Ill.: Tyndale House, 1987.
   1. Future life—Biblical teaching. 2. Future life—
Christianity. I. Title.
BS680.F83B39   1997   236—dc21   96-46396
                                                                          CIP

ISBN 0-8254-2158-6

Printed in the United States of America

1 2 3 / 03 02 01 00 99 98 97

*With warm esteem these pages are dedicated to
the reverend doctor Harvey D. McCarty, for
over twenty-two years beloved minister of
University Baptist Church, Fayetteville,
Arkansas; chaplain of the Arkansas
"Razorbacks"; formerly State Chairman of the
Fellowship of Christian Athletes; Chaplain
(Brigadier General) in the Air National Guard
of the United States; also to his gifted wife,
Shirley, than whom no minister of
the Gospel ever had a truer helpmeet,
counselor, and complement.*

CONTENTS

FOREWORD

No apology need ever be made for publishing an honest contribution to the subject of death and the Beyond. However big and pressing the questions related to our present short life on earth may seem, they shrink into littleness compared with this timeless, measureless concern of death and the vast hereafter. How long earthly life looks to questing youth! How quickly fled it seems to the aged! The grandfather clock ticks away the minutes so slowly, but in retrospect the years seem to have scurried away like dust before a gale. No matter how wise a man may think himself, if he neglects to enquire as to the long, long journey which he must soon take on the other side of death he is a fool. That millions of people can treat the matter with jaunty indifference must be an astonishment to angels and demons.

There are other reasons why no apology is ever needed for a treatise on death and the Beyond. While millions show little interest, others are deeply concerned but are misdirected, perplexed, or deceived by untrue teachings. Cults and "isms" spread plausible errors about life the other side of death, while many of us evangelicals seem too busy with other issues to give truly biblical answers.

The following pages are at least one attempt to clarify what the Bible teaches on life after death, and at the same time to answer some widespread errors. Our contribution may be unpretentious but it is sincere and is written with cordial respect for all those whose theories we are obliged to criticize. May truth, and truth alone, prevail.

J. S. B.

ONE

AN AFTERLIFE: YES OR NO?

This life, which baffles him who seeks to find
   The why and wherefore of its source and end,
Most well deserves the thought of our whole mind,
   To learn whereto its passing phases tend:
Though it be wrapped in clouds of mystery,
   And men oft wonder whence they came and why,
There is for each one solemn certainty,
   It is that life is transient: *all must die.*

Anonymous

Life is real, life is earnest,
   And the grave is not its goal:
"Dust thou art, to dust returnest,"
   Was not spoken of the soul.

Henry Wadsworth Longfellow

Is death a fear or worry to people nowadays? There are those who say "No. We have discarded belief in life beyond the grave." But I learn from a group of psychiatrists that seven or eight out of every ten persons who come to them are haunted, disturbed, and in some cases almost demented by apprehensiveness of death and the Beyond.

The many people who shrug off any mention of death, professing themselves too modern to be scared, are self-deluded. Their seeming bravery is mere bravado. I have known some such individuals, and have seen their super-ciliousness turn to terror when at last death got its icy stranglehold on them.

Death is a stark reality. It can neither be halted nor cheated. Our wisdom is to face it. The ostrich policy is futile. Is there any authentic source of information as to what lies on the other side of death? That is a question no one needs be ashamed to ask; and it leads to a further question.

What is the most vital question in our country today? Has it to do with the political, the commercial, the international? Many people would judge so. Not one in a thousand will readily concur, but the most urgent question in

America today is the inspiration and authority of the Bible. America was built on the Bible. The founding fathers may not have been right in all their interpretations of it, nor in all their applications of it, but in the main they were so. The national constitution which they hammered into shape was Bible-based. Upon that foundation America became the greatest nation on earth. If America remains true to that Book, it will continue to be great; but if it listens to our present-day Bible-detractors and plays the renegade, it will decay. Samson will lose his great strength. He will be blinded and find himself grinding in the prison-house of the Communist Philistines.

This is the biggest of all questions: Is the Bible truly the supernaturally inspired Word of God? If it is, then we have *certainty*—certainty about God, about origins, about morals, about man, about our race's future, and about human destiny on the other side of death. But if the Bible is anything less than that (let us be blunt), we do not have certainty about any of those most fundamental of all issues. We are only groping and guessing. No other book ever made such impressive claims to be authoritatively inspired by the one true God; nor did any other book ever give such scientifically testable evidences of being thus inspired. In the long run (or perhaps not so long) America will either prosper or wither according to its loyalty toward that Book.

It is outside our present scope to furnish proofs that the Bible is indeed the authentic Word of God. Many books have been written on that subject by able Christian apologists. The credentials of the Bible, in my judgment, are ample to convince any open mind. Therefore, as we here enquire concerning the other side of death, the Bible is our final court of appeal. As for beliefs *outside* the Bible, I make no more than this one comprehensive comment. Varied and intensive investigation indicates that belief in an afterlife has existed more or less definitely, in one form or another, among all known races from the beginning of history. Differing ideas of it have been affected considerably by geographical circumstances and by degree of civilization. Concepts have been vague or sensuous or fanciful, and in some instances ghastly; but the belief itself seems a basic intuition of human nature. As we review those many ideas, from the dawn of time to the end of the B.C. centuries, we may well be grateful for the authentic revelation which has been given to us in the Bible. The sun has risen. Why creep amid the dark shadows? At last we have certainty; for we have the inspired Word of the only true and living God.

WHAT ABOUT ABOUT MODERN COMMUNISM?

What of Communism and its denial of an afterlife? Our reply is unhesitating. Never before has there been such a reverting to childhood mentality as the Communist aberration that the mind or soul is only a combination of atoms like all the other parts of us. Unthinkable as it is to suppose that the gigantic physical universe created itself before itself existed, or that it evolved without direction out of sheer nothing, it is even more absurd to pretend that senseless matter created thinking mind or somehow evolved it. That a supreme *Mind* created the universe is easy and sensible to believe, but to argue that blank nothing evolved matter, and that inanimate matter produced human *intellect,* is surely philosophizing gone mad.

Matter can be analyzed right down to the microscopic, but what microscope can see *mind?* What chemistry can define *thought?* How did such abstract realities as love, hate, hope, fear, joy, sorrow, develop from insensible matter, even if we regard matter as pure electrical charges rather than physical particles? Even more, how did physical atoms or electrical waves produce *conscience* in man, with a deep consciousness of moral accountability?

If the mind, like the body, is only matter, it should age and weaken as the body ages and weakens. How is it, then, that the mind often grows most mature and vigorous when the body, by the usual wear-and-tear process, is declining to the grave? Often indeed, when the body is most wasted by disease, the mind is most alert. All such considerations confirm that mind is not mere matter.

Physiologists tell us that by the end of every seven years (some say three) every particle of our bodies has changed. So a man forty-nine years old, although his body remains organically the same, has actually had seven bodies (or sixteen). It follows, therefore, that if the mind also is matter it must have undergone a similar transmutation process. But that would mean a change of self-consciousness and of the thinking *person*. There would be no recollection of the past, for all the memory particles have given place to others, and all the earlier identity particles are no longer there! In a mental and personal sense, that man of forty-nine would not be the same man. Such an idea, of course, reduces thought to the ridiculous.

Recently I heard a radio program in which a distinguished Russian author was asked, "Is it true that there is unrest among Russian youth today, a tiredness with Communist atheism, and a movement back to belief in God?" The reply was definite. There is, and the Kremlin is concerned about it. That reply need not surprise us. Even the Kremlin cannot destroy that which is the deepest innate intuition of our human constitution. Many Communist jailers in Russian prison camps who have been converted to the Christian faith have later confessed that during their most blatant days of Communism and professed atheism they knew, deep down, that God *is,* and that there is a Judgment Day in the Beyond.

In this physical microcosm, the human body, every time the heart beats there are molecules by the millions dissolved and replaced. Yet you and I know that despite this unremitting process of chemical change we are the same persons from our first baby breath until now. The mind, the soul, that nonmaterial, indefinable substance which is the real you, the real me, outlives all physical change, thereby challenging us to believe that it will outlive that final change which we call death.

We may go further and say that belief in a future life seems to be an *inborn necessity* of human nature. It is truly said that to the lower animals "the present is everything." Those household pets do no planning for the future, nor do the denizens of the jungle. They live entirely in the "now." Not so do human beings. The *future* is what we live for. The present is always seen as leading to something further. As we draw near the close of our mortal years we feel that there *must* be some answering future beyond the earthly. Those who have had a hard, painful, frustrating time here feel that there ought to be a compensation there. Those with special gifts, and those who have spent themselves pursuing high ideals, scientific studies, and altruistic aims, instinctively feel that there must surely be an after-death continuity which sublimates them. Equally so, most who have lived in willful wickedness cannot stamp out of their degenerated moral system the disturbing conviction that there must be a day of reckoning.

No, this idea of an afterlife is no artificial implant. It is a constitutional ingredient of human nature. It may be ignored for a time, plausibly explained away, angrily put aside, but it ineradicably persists. It may be buried beneath much earthly philosophy, but again and again it resurrects itself. There may be odd exceptions, but they only prove the rule. It has always been like that. It always will be.

Death is still on the rampage. Through the centuries men have seen bodies die, but nobody ever saw a soul die. No one has ever yet been able to supply evidence that the real man, the spiritual soul, disintegrates. Nor has anyone been able to give proof that the soul does *not* live on hereafter.

However, we need linger no longer with merely human

reasoning. We have, at last, a final court of appeal: the Bible, the inspired Word of God; and to that greatest Book on earth we now turn.

TWO

THE BIBLICAL TEACHING IN GENERAL

In planning these studies I had to decide which would be the best order of approach. At first I thought the best way would be to answer and dispose of certain *erroneous* theories supposedly based on the Bible. It soon became evident, however, that such a procedure would be too long, tedious, and negative. Therefore I begin by giving a general outline of what I believe is the true teaching of the Bible on the subject. Some will disagree. Those who hold Seventh-Day Adventist or Bullinger theories of "soul sleep," for instance, will diverge from what we say here about sheol, hades, paradise, and the intermediate state. I believe they are wrong: but all such points at which there are likely variances of interpretation will be carefully considered later.

J. S. B.

Our subject is the Bible and the Beyond. What does the Bible teach about the other side of death? As an introduction I quote from the Book of Job, chapter 14, verse 10: "Man giveth up the ghost, and where is he?"

Although the Book of Genesis comes first in our Bible, it may not have been the first to be written. There are cogent reasons for believing that the Book of Job is of even greater antiquity. What a remarkable product the Book of Job is! It may possibly be the oldest writing in known literature, yet the problems with which it deals are as up to date in our human pathos as if it had come from the printing press last week. Some of the profoundest questions ever raised are found in that old poetic debate; questions concerning providence and the divine government of mankind; concerning human responsibility, right and wrong, sickness and suffering, death and the Beyond. Some of those questions, as they now come to us through our dear old King James Version of the Bible, are garbed in wording which sounds quaint to some modern ears; yet they are singularly arresting. One such is that which I have just quoted: "Man giveth up the ghost, and where is he?"

Job's question has echoed in the minds of the thoughtful

through every generation. Death is man's monster problem. There certainly is no room to doubt the dismal fact that "man giveth up the ghost." A million graveyards proclaim with ceaseless voice that man is mortal and that the living are dying. What wreckage of the race has Death made! The earth is full of the bones of the dead. What is this revolving orb on which we live but the vast cemetery of mankind? There is no retarding the grim-faced marauder. He stalks among thrones as well as in cottages. Oft his fell stroke is as unanticipated as it is inexorable. He is no respecter of persons. The shadow of his ebon scepter falls alike on princes and beggars. He is ever with us, and ever busy. As the pen of poetry puts it, "Life's gaudy stage is but an inch above the grave." As the Anglican liturgy words it, "In the midst of life we are in death." Even amid the silver bells of the wedding day there sounds the muffled knell, "Till death us do part."

With insatiable appetite, death calls daily for millions at a meal. Some sixty or seventy persons per minute is the world's average death rate, which means that for every tick of the clock some human soul is passing from this present life on earth into—well, into what? Where? Surely there is something strangely incongruous about those many people who never bother to inquire what their ultimate destiny is in that mysterious "other side of death."

But what answer shall we give to those many others who are concerned to know about that "other side"? Where shall wisdom be found? From the wisest sages of antiquity, on through the brilliant days of the Greek philosophers, down to the ablest reasoners of today, one looks in vain for any clear and convincing answer from the unaided intellect of man. Vagueness, grotesqueness, uncertainty, silence, or confessed ignorance are the marks of merely human teachers in relation to the Beyond.

Is there any *authoritative* source of information? There is. In this present enquiry it is outside our scope to furnish

22

arguments that the Bible is the supernaturally inspired Word of God. Able treatises on that subject have been published by front-rank apologists. Suffice it here to say that there are ample proofs and credentials to satisfy any honest enquirer. What, then, does the *Bible* teach about life after death?

THE FACT OF AN AFTERLIFE

First, the Bible asserts the *fact* of an afterlife. To give all the references would be to quote from practically every part of the Bible, which I cannot do here. I simply quote two texts as samples of the many. The first is Hebrews 9:27: "It is appointed unto men once to die, but after this the judgment." The other is John 5:28-29, where our Lord Jesus says, "The hour is coming, in the which all that are in the graves shall hear his voice [i.e., his own voice], and shall come forth; they that have done good unto the resurrection of life; and they that have done evil unto the resurrection of condemnation."

The Bible is by no means alone in thus asserting the fact of an afterlife. All religions worth even a passing glance, whether they are extinct or extant, teach an afterlife in one form or another.

THE SPHERES OF THE AFTERLIFE

Second, in considerable degree the Bible reveals the *spheres* of the afterlife. Often it is glibly caricatured in that connection. It is said to teach that at death all the good go to heaven, and all the bad go to hell; or that when Christians die they go to their final reward, and when others die they go to their final doom. Yet the Bible does *not* teach so; and since the Bible is the Word of God, how careful we should be not to misrepresent it! As one step toward clarification, let me read our Lord's words about the rich man and Lazarus, as recorded in Luke 16:19-31. I quote from the King James Version.

There was a certain rich man, which was clothed in purple and fine linen, and fared sumptuously every day: and there was a certain beggar named Lazarus, which was laid at his gate, full of sores, and desiring to be fed with the crumbs which fell from the rich man's table: moreover the dogs came and licked his sores. And it came to pass, that the beggar died, and was carried by the angels into Abraham's bosom: the rich man also died, and was buried; and in *hell* he lift up his eyes, being in torments, and seeth Abraham afar off, and Lazarus in his bosom. And he cried and said, Father Abraham, have mercy on me, and send Lazarus, that he may dip the tip of his finger in water, and cool my tongue; for I am tormented in this flame. But Abraham said, Son, remember that thou in thy lifetime receivedst thy good things, and likewise Lazarus evil things: but now he is comforted, and thou art tormented. And beside all this, between us and you there is a great gulf fixed: so that they which would pass from hence to you cannot; neither can they pass to us, that would come from thence. Then he said, I pray thee therefore, father, that thou wouldest send him to my father's house: for I have five brethren; that he may testify unto them, lest they also come into this place of torment. Abraham saith unto him, They have Moses and the prophets; let them hear them. And he said, Nay, father Abraham: but if one went unto them from the dead, they will repent. And he [Abraham] said unto him, If they hear not Moses and the prophets, neither will they be persuaded, though one rose from the dead.

Observe that the rich man, immediately after his death, was in "hell." If we are rightly to apprehend what the Bible teaches about post-mortem existence, we must understand its usage of the word *hell*. How many hundred times does that word occur in the Bible? To hear some uninformed critics talk, one would think it comes on every page and in every paragraph. "Oh, that's the book which is full of hell-fire," they say. Well, it certainly is the Book which warns us of it; but the truth is, the Bible is as sparing as possible in its use of the word *hell*. It does not use it even one hundred times. In all its 66 books and 1,189 chapters of the Bible, the word is used only 54 times. Even allowing for variant translations of the Hebrew and Greek words which are usually rendered as *hell* in our English Bible, the full total is only 88.*

This, then, is the first fact to grasp. In our English Bible the word *hell* occurs 54 times. Of those 54 occurrences, 31 are found in the Old Testament, and 23 in the New. Yes, mark those numbers carefully: in the entire Bible, 54; in the Old Testament, 31; in the New Testament, 23.

As for the Old Testament, in all 31 places where the word *hell* is used, the Hebrew word, without exception, is *sheol*. That word is also translated as "grave" 31 times, and as "pit" 3 times. So altogether *sheol* appears 65 times.

THAT HEBREW WORD *SHEOL*

What does that Hebrew word *sheol* signify? The first guide to its meaning is that in all of its occurrences it is never used in the plural. That is because it does not refer merely to the grave dug in the earth, but to that which lies *beyond*, of which the grave is the symbol, and to which it is the gloomy portal. Whenever the Hebrews wished to refer only to the grave in the earth where the body lies, they had another word, *qeber*, and that is why, wherever we find *graves* (plural) the Hebrew word is *qeber*.

Some have tried to establish that the word *sheol* means no more than the grave. Therefore it is important to note the difference between *sheol* and *qeber*. The word *qeber* is always used to denote *only* the burial place of the body. If more than that is intended, *sheol* is used. *Qeber* is the grave as dug by man and owned by man. *Sheol* is never thus

---

*Actually, the word *hell* should not be in our English Bible at all. It does not truly represent either the Old Testament *sheol* or the New Testament *hades* and *gehenna*. In early English it had a quite innocuous meaning, but for approximately the last two hundred years it has meant one thing only, the fiery damnation of the wicked after their death on earth. It would have been far better if the words *sheol* and *hades* and *gehenna* had been left untranslated and simply lifted just as they are from the Hebrew and the Greek. In fact, most recent translations *do* that with the word *hades*. What I emphasize is that hell as a never-ending fire-torment to which evildoers go immediately after death does *not* truly represent any of those three words in the original.

used. It cannot be dug by man or owned by man. In those occurrences of *sheol* where the emphasis seems to indicate that the grave is referred to, our translators have faithfully rendered *sheol* as "grave"; but where it plainly indicates the mysterious Beyond, they have translated it as "hell." So then, let us grasp this clearly: *sheol* is the Old Testament word for the Beyond. Also, wherever the word *hell* occurs in our English Old Testament, without exception *sheol* is the Hebrew word behind it.

THE NEW TESTAMENT WORDS

As for the New Testament, our word *hell* does *not* always represent the same Greek word. Of its 23 occurrences, 10 times the Greek word is *hades,* and 12 times it is *gehenna.* But to those 10 occurrences of *hades* we must add 1 Corinthians 15:55, where *hades* is translated as "grave"—"O grave [hades], where is thy victory?" Also, in 2 Peter 2:4, where the King James Version says that God "cast down to *hell"* the "angels that sinned," the word *hell* should be changed to *tartarus* (the deeper abyss of hades).

So, in the 23 occurrences of *hell* in the English New Testament, 12 times it is *gehenna;* 10 times *hades;* and once *tartarus* (which make the 23). And to those we must add that one other reference to hades in 1 Corinthians 15:55, "O *hades,* where is thy victory?" Those are the simple data; but one needs to know in each text whether the word is *hades* or *gehenna,* for they represent *two different places.* Here are the texts where they occur. *Hades:* Matthew 11:23; 16:18; Luke 10:15; 16:23; Acts 2:27, 31; 1 Corinthians 15:55 (translated "grave"); 2 Peter 2:4 (tartarus); Revelation 1:18; 6:8; 20:13-14. *Gehenna:* Matthew 5:22, 29-30; 10:28; 18:9; 23:15, 33; Mark 9:43, 45, 47; Luke 12:5; James 3:6.

As for the etymology of the two words: *Hades* means simply the place that is *unseen,* or at least unseeable to bodily eyes. *Gehenna* signifies the *Gorge of Hinnom,* a deep ravine near Jerusalem, where in former times human sacrifices were offered (2 Chron. 33:6; Jer. 7:31), and where, in New Testament times, both animal and human carcasses, along with the city garbage, were dumped for burning, where the fire was never quenched, and from which the obnoxious fumes continually ascended. Perhaps it is not surprising that *gehenna* gradually became used to symbolize the final doom of the impenitent wicked.

To underline this, let me quote a graphic comment from *Salvator Mundi,* a book now long out of print, by the late Samuel Cox.

As to the derivation of the word, there is not, there never has been, the slightest doubt. *Gehenna* is the Greek form of the Hebrew *Ge-Hinnom,* or "Valley of Hinnom." This valley was a steep ravine immediately under the south-western wall of Jerusalem, watered by the brook Kidron and "Siloa's sacred stream." In the time of the Hebrew kings it was laid out in paradises, i.e., pleasure gardens with their groves, pools, and fishponds. Here the wealthier nobles and citizens of Jerusalem had their country villas, their summer palaces. At its south-eastern extremity lay the paradise of King Solomon, with its "tophet," or music grove, the grove in which the king, with his wives and concubines, listened to his men-singers and women-singers and to the blended strains of "musical instruments of divers sorts."

The whole beautiful valley, in short, was full of those delicious retreats which are still found in the close neighbourhood of large and wealthy Oriental cities, and in which the monarch and his nobles have sought repose from the sultry heat of the summer and from the frets and toils of public life.

To gratify the foreign women with whom he consorted, Solomon polluted his pleasant gardens and groves with idolatrous shrines in which the cruel and licentious rites of Egypt and Phoenicia were observed. His successors imitated and outran his evil example. The horrid fires of Molech were kindled in the beautiful valley, and children were burned in them—"passed through the fire." Gradually "the valley of Hinnom" grew to be a type of all that was flagrantly wicked and abominable to the faithful souls, fallen on evil times, who still worshiped Jehovah on the neighbouring hill of Zion. And when Josiah came to the throne, and good men could once more lift up their heads, the groves were burned down, the pleasant gardens laid waste, the shrines ground to powder; and, to render the valley forever un-

27

clean, the bones of the dead were strewn over its surface. Thenceforth it became the common cesspool of the city, into which offal was cast, and the carcasses of animals, and even the bodies of great criminals who had lived a life so vile as to be judged unworthy of decent burial. Worms preyed on their corrupting flesh; and fires were kept burning lest the pestilential infection should rise from the valley and float through the streets of Jerusalem.

To the Hebrew prophets this foul, terrible valley became an apt type or illustration of the doom of the unrighteous. They drew from it their images . . . of the worm that never dies, and of the fire which is not quenched. To say that a man was in danger of Gehenna was to say that his sins had exposed him to a judgment the terrors of which were faintly shadowed forth by the sickening horrors of the detestable Ge-Hinnom.

So then, in the New Testament *gehenna* is used to prefigure the final doom of the lost. On the other hand, *hades* is never used with that meaning. It is revealed as the sphere of departed souls *between* the death of the body here on earth and the yet-future Day of Judgment. The *hades* of the New Testament and the *sheol* of the Old Testament are identical, though of course there is fuller and clearer teaching in the New Testament than in the Old.

There are still Christian ministers, more than a few, who vaguely assume unquestioningly that *gehenna* is simply an alternative name for *hades*—that both hades and gehenna are one and the same place of punishment to which the dissolute go after leaving this earth. They are wrong. When our Lord warned against being condemned to gehenna, to the "fire unquenchable" (Mark 9:43, 45, 57) he certainly was not meaning any merely temporary hades. Nor was he when he said, "Fear him who . . . has power to cast unto gehenna" (Luke 12:5), for no such "power" is needed to cast men only into hades, seeing that all human beings go there as a matter of course when death disembodies them. The Jews had some strange ideas about gehenna, but they seem to have been all one in this, that gehenna signified to them the final fate of the godless and impenitent in the Beyond.

Once for all, get hold of the distinction between *hades* and *gehenna*. Always remember that hades is the place of intermediate detention between the grave and the coming general judgment of mankind at the Great White Throne; whereas gehenna is the final doom of the damned.

Now here is the first big, crucial fact to note. *The Bible nowhere says that at the death of the body any soul goes immediately to that final gehenna. It plainly conveys that all the departed (except born-again Christians) are in hades until the yet-future general judgment.* That, of course sets us asking: What about hades, the detention-sphere of disembodied human souls between now and that final Judgment Day? Does Scripture give us information on that? It does.

HADES, A PLACE OF CONSCIOUSNESS

Reverting to Luke 16, we find that hades is a place of *consciousness.* Note our Lord's words about the "rich man" who died and then awoke in "hell." You will hardly need telling that the Greek word there translated as "hell" is *hades.* Yes, he was in hades; and what does our Lord say of him?

1. "In hades he lift up his eyes"—so he could *see.*
2. "Being in torments"—so he could *feel.*
3. "And seeth Abraham . . . Lazarus"—so he could *recognize.*
4. "He cried and said . . ."—so he could *speak.*
5. "Abraham, have mercy . . ."—so he could *plead.*
6. "I am tormented in this flame"—so he could *suffer.*
7. "Abraham said [to him]"—so he could *hear.*
8. "Son, remember . . ."—so he had *memory.*
9. "Send to my . . . brethren"—so he could *reflect.*
10. "Lest they also come . . ."—so he could *think ahead.*

Thus our Lord gives us tenfold evidence of continuing consciousness in hades. That disembodied condition neither extinguishes nor diminishes human consciousness, but rather intensifies it. Nor is that lifting of the curtain on hades the only Scripture where hades is shown to be a place of both self-awareness and other-awareness; though even that one clear utterance from our omniscient Lord should suffice to settle the matter.

THE "GREAT GULF" OF HADES

Hades is shown, also, to be divided into two main parts; the one part, spoken of as "Abraham's bosom," being separated from the other by an impassable "great gulf." Thus we see that the separation between the godly and the ungodly, between the believer and the unbeliever, not only persists beyond the grave, but becomes there deep-fixed.

What is meant by "Abraham's bosom"? The expression is used in the Jewish Talmud, which gathers together in its encyclopedic contents ages of authentic Jewish tradition and teaching. It is used as synonymous with another Talmudic term, i.e., "Paradise." In Jewish theology "Abraham's bosom" or "Paradise" was that part of hades (or sheol) where the departed and disembodied godly or righteous awaited future resurrection. When hanging on the Cross, our Lord Jesus said to the penitent malefactor, "To day shalt thou be with me in *paradise"*; and that remorseful criminal knew at once what our Lord meant. (More on this later.) When our Savior vacated his crucified body and left it hanging as a corpse on the Cross, he immediately passed in disembodied condition into the "paradise" or "Abraham's bosom" part of hades. That is what is meant when we recite those words in the Apostles' Creed, "He descended into hell." I am glad to see that in some recent editions of the Apostles' Creed the word *hell* has been replaced by the word *hades*.

What of the numberless "heathen" who have died without ever hearing the Gospel or learning about the true God? Have they all gone to a final state of doom? The Bible nowhere teaches so. They all abide in hades until the "appointed" day on which God will "judge the world in righteousness."

What of the many millions through the centuries in our

own so-called "Christian countries" who, although they have heard the Gospel many a time, have never intelligently grasped it, and have died without knowing Christ savingly? Have they already gone to a final damnation? Our Bible does not teach so. They, too, are in hades, detained there in disembodied humanhood until "the judgment of the great day."

What about the *fallen angels* of whom we read in Holy Writ, those originally sinless spirit-intelligences who, strangely enough, ages ago, "kept not their first estate" but left "their own habitation"? They, too, are in hades, in its deeper darkness called *tartarus*. Listen to 2 Peter 2:4 and Jude verse 6.

> God spared not the angels that sinned, but cast them down to *tartarus* [deepest abyss of hades], and delivered them into chains of darkness, to be reserved unto judgment.
> The angels which kept not their first estate, but left their own habitation, he hath reserved in everlasting chains under darkness unto the judgment of the great day.

Yes, in their millions, all *non*believers (those who have never known the Gospel) and all *un*believers (those who have known it and rejected it) and even all those fallen angels are now in hades, and will be there until the vast assize at the Great White Throne.

HADES, A PRISON

Another thing which Scripture makes clear is that although hades is not the place of final doom it is a grim *prison,* especially for unbelievers and impenitent wicked-doers. In the Old Testament we find such expressions as "the *gates* of sheol," and the "*power* of sheol." Also, in Isaiah's startling passage about the humiliating deposition of Lucifer down to sheol, we find sheol called "the house of his *prisoners.*"

See King Hezekiah's lament in Isaiah 38:10: "I shall go to the *gates* of sheol." Note Jehovah's word in Hosea 13:14: "I will ransom them from the *power* of sheol." And let me quote that dramatic paragraph just referred to about the expulsion of Lucifer from his pristine dignity:

> Sheol from beneath is moved for thee to meet thee at thy coming: it stirreth up the dead for thee. . . . Thy pomp is brought down to sheol. . . . How art thou fallen from heaven, O Lucifer, son of the morning! . . . Thou shalt be brought down to sheol, to the sides of the pit. . . . Is this the man who made the earth to tremble, who shook kingdoms; who made the world as a wilderness, and destroyed the cities thereof; who opened not the house of his prisoners? (Isa. 14:9, 11-12, 15-17)

Those Old Testament expressions—"gates" and "power" and "prisoners"—have their New Testament counterparts. In Matthew 16:18 our Lord Jesus mentions those "gates" of hades when he says, "Upon this Rock I will build my church; and the *gates* of hades shall not prevail against it." I have heard some strange sermons on those words. Our Lord is supposed to have meant that his church would be a militant church; an attacking, conquering army which even the gates of hades would not be able to withstand. He meant no such thing. Who on earth wants to storm the gate of hades and get inside there? You can leave me out of any army wanting to break into that vault of gloom! What our Lord meant was not that his church should storm hades, but that the "gates of hades" would never prevail to hold prisoner any blood-bought member of his true Church. Thank God, hades never has and never will hold any of his people prisoner; for as 2 Corinthians 5:8 says, when Christians die, "to be absent from the body" is to be "present with the Lord."

But besides our Lord's reference to the "gates" of hades, the New Testament speaks about the "power" of hades and of the "prisoners" in it. Hebrews 2:14 tells us that God the Son became incarnate so that through death he might destroy him that had the *power* of death, that is, the *devil*. And in 1 Peter 3:19 we are told about the "spirits in *prison*" which were disobedient in the days of Noah.

32

OUR LORD AND HADES

That brings us to a most vital consideration. Christ himself has been down into hades; and the Scriptures plainly convey to us that his resurrection from hades and his ascension to heaven have wrought a tremendous change in that part of hades called "Abraham's bosom" or "paradise." Let me quote 1 Peter 3:18-19 more fully:

> For Christ also hath once suffered for sins, the just for the unjust, that he might bring us to God, being put to death in the flesh, but quickened by the Spirit: by which also he went and preached unto the spirits in prison.

There has been no little speculation as to the meaning of that text. What did our disembodied Lord "preach" to those "spirits" in that "prison"? The Greek word seems to mean that he preached the Gospel—which is confirmed by 1 Peter 4:6: "For this cause was the *gospel* preached also to them that are dead, that they might be judged according to men in the flesh, but live according to God in the spirit." So, did our Lord preach the Gospel to them with a view to their conversion and salvation? Hardly, for Peter clearly says, "that they might be *judged*," which means that they are going to the final Judgment Day. Does it suggest that on the other side of the grave there is a so-called "second chance" for departed souls to be saved? Well, remember this: those "spirits in prison" had never before heard the Gospel even once, so they were not being given a "*second chance*" to hear it. Also remember that they were disembodied wicked-doers who had lived on earth before the Noachian Flood, eight hundred years before God gave the *law* through Moses. As Romans 4:15 says, "Where no law is, there is no transgression." So although they were indeed sinners, they were not "transgressors" in the same way as those who later disobeyed a God-given *law*. Much of their sin was in ignorance. There, for the moment, we must leave that matter and come back to the great *change* which our Lord's resurrection and ascension made upon the "paradise" part of hades. In Ephesians 4:8-10 Paul writes:

When he [Christ] ascended up on high, he led captivity captive, and gave gifts unto men. (Now that he ascended, what is it but that he also descended first into the lower parts of the earth? He that descended is the same also that ascended up far above all heavens, that he might fill all things.)

That phrase, "the lower parts of the earth," would be understood at once by Paul's first readers to mean hades. The identical phrase occurs in Psalm 63:9 where it refers undoubtedly to sheol or hades. Our Lord Jesus used a practically identical phrase when he said, "As Jonas was three days and three nights in the whale's belly; so shall the Son of man be three days and three nights in the heart of the earth." No one would argue that by "the heart of the earth" our Lord meant no more than the sepulchre in which his corpse was deposited. Nay, Jonah himself, speaking of his experience inside the fish, said, "Out of the belly of sheol [hades] cried I." Our Lord meant that just as Jonah had gone into hades *symbolically,* so he himself would go there *actually.* Neither our Lord nor Paul meant that hades is a "lower part" inside the solid earth itself. They meant that the grave, deep-dug in the earth, *represented* that unseen "deep" which lies just beyond. But to clinch the matter, we know that they meant hades, for Scripture tells us plainly that our Lord actually went there.

So, see now what his descent there *did.* In Paul's Ephesian epistle, chapter 4, he says that our Lord, on vacating hades, "led captivity captive." What does that mean? Well, for one thing, it means that he took captive the *place* of captivity itself. He became the *Master* of hades and of all the millions imprisoned there. Moreover, he now became the *Liberator* from hades of all those godly souls in their thousands who, while on earth, had lived and died in the faith of Abraham. In Romans 4:11 Abraham is called "the father of all them that believe." All true believers during the Old Testament era who, as Hebrews 11:13 says, "died in faith, not having received the promises, but having seen them afar off," were gathered in sheol or hades to "Abraham's bosom," awaiting with him the coming triumph of the promised Messiah.

Look again at those words, "He led captivity captive." That is how it reads in the King James Version; but practically all recent versions render it more or less identically as: "He led forth a host of captives." Who, then, were that multitude of captives whom our Lord led out from hades up to heaven in the train of his triumph? They certainly were not those evil spirits who are confederates of Satan. *They* were left down there where they belong. Nor were they the millions of the ungodly, the unbelieving, the corrupt-minded in hades. *They* have no place in heaven. That multitude of "captives" whom our Lord swept up from hades to the third heaven with himself must have been the godly seed of Abraham. Get the picture? Just as victorious generals of long ago used to ride in their chariots through the city with their multitude of prisoners dragging behind in wretched display, so Jesus, the victorious "captain of our salvation," led his "host of captives" behind his shining chariot. The one big difference between him and all other conquerors was that *his* grateful "captives" were led *out* of slavery, not into it.

What a thrilling disclosure is that emancipation from hades! No wonder Jesus said, "Abraham rejoiced to see my day: and he saw it and was glad" (John 8:56). No wonder inspired David exclaimed, "Thou wilt not leave my soul in sheol" (Ps. 16:10). When Christ rose and ascended, the gates were flung open. The "Abraham's bosom" area of hades was evacuated, or, rather, was transferred with all its occupants to where the risen Christ now is.

There is interesting confirmation of this in other parts of the New Testament. In 2 Corinthians 12:2 Paul writes, "I knew a man in Christ above fourteen years ago . . . caught up to the *third heaven.*" In the next verse but one he varies the wording and says, "caught up into *paradise"* (v. 4). Those two terms, "the third heaven" and "paradise," are synonymous, which means that paradise is no longer the "Abraham's bosom" area of hades; it has been transferred to the "third heaven."

What then, is the "third heaven"? Well, in that Ephesian passage which we quoted a moment ago, Paul says that our Lord Jesus "ascended above *all* heavens." So there is a plurality of heavens besides that highest of all heavens which, in a concentrated way, is the abode of God. There are those who say that the three heavens are (1) the lower heaven of the clouds, (2) the vaster heaven of the stars, and (3) the "heaven of heavens," the abode of God. I will not flatly deny that such may be the meaning, but I much doubt it. Paul was referring to spirit-*spheres,* not to physical layers. This much, however, is radiantly certain: that "third heaven" is where, in some sublime way, our Lord Jesus now is, and where the presence of God is more immediately realized.

WHAT OF CHRISTIANS AFTER DEATH?

That naturally leads to the question: What, then, of Christian believers when *they* die? The Scriptures give us a clear answer. True Christian believers do *not* go to hades, not even to that part called "paradise"; for paradise is no longer there; it has been transferred to that "third heaven" where Christ now is. Therefore, when true Christians depart from the mortal body, in their case, as 2 Corinthians 5:8 says, "To be absent from the body, [is] to be *present with the Lord."* No hades for the Christian, but an immediate rapture into the paradise of our Lord's presence!

Complemental to that, Scripture reveals another big development which may well evoke our wonder and gratitude. Our Lord Jesus, through his death and resurrection, has wrested the *power* of hades from the devil's grasp. Not only did he liberate thousands of the archfiend's prisoners, he deprived him of the *keys;* for when he appeared to John on the Isle of Patmos he declared, "I am the living one; and I became dead, and behold, I am alive unto the ages of the ages, and I have the *keys* of death and of *hades!*" (Rev. 1:18). Yes, thank God, the keys of hades are now in those nail-pierced hands!

At the second coming of Christ, those who are now with him in that third-heaven paradise will return to earth with him, at which time they will suddenly find themselves clothed with their resurrection bodies. Simultaneously, Christians then alive on earth will be changed "in the twinkling of an eye," and they too will experience the instant ecstasy of physical metamorphosis into undecaying youth. In our millions we shall "meet the Lord in the air." And what is the first thing that will happen then? We shall all break into singing a mighty song which will reverberate round the shining skies. Paul has told us in advance what that glory-song will be, in 1 Corinthians 15:54-55.

> DEATH IS SWALLOWED UP IN VICTORY.
> O DEATH, WHERE IS THY STING?
> O *HADES*, WHERE IS THY VICTORY?

Yes, "O Hades, where is thy victory?" That will be the culminating demonstration of our Lord's declaration, "Upon this rock I will build my church; and the *gates of hades* shall not prevail against it." Not one of all our Savior's redeemed millions will be a prisoner behind those "gates of hades." In utter victory over mortality and hades we shall share our Lord's millennial kingdom and, after that, serve and adore him forever amid the deathless felicities of the New Jerusalem.

WHAT OF NON-CHRISTIANS AFTER DEATH?

But what of those who live and die without Christ? Let our answer to that question be given with solemn cautiousness. As we have already said, at their demise they pass as disembodied souls into hades, the place of intermediate detention between the death of the body and the future "Day of Judgment." Even during our Lord's coming millennial reign on earth there will still be death here; and those who die then, just as those who die now, will pass into hades to await the final day of reckoning. Then, *after* the Millennium, after the last insurrection of evil on this earth and its final abolition, and after the ultimate doom of Satan has been effected, the Great White Throne of the supreme divine inquisition will be set, and all the multi-millions of the departed shall then come forth from hades to be judged. That awesome day of destiny is graphically described in Revelation 20:11-15.

> And I saw a great white throne, and him that sat on it, from whose face the earth and the heaven fled away; and there was found no place for them. And I saw the dead, small and great, stand before God; and the books were opened: and another book was opened which is the book of life: and the dead were judged out of those things which were written in the books, according to their works. And the sea gave up the dead which were in it; and death and *hades* delivered up the dead which were in them; and they were judged every man according to their works. And death and hades were cast into the lake of fire. This is the second death. And whosoever was not found written in the book of life was cast into the lake of fire.

What an unparalleled scene of dread that apocalyptic vision pictures to us! See death and hades at last disgorge their aggregate millions. The wording is clear: "Death and hades delivered up the dead which were in them." The grave delivers up the *bodies* it has claimed; and hades delivers up the *souls* it has imprisoned. Bodies and souls will be reunited for the purpose of that fateful tribunal. Does someone exclaim, "Impossible! How could all those numberless bodies be raised which have disintegrated into nonexistence?" The answer is that it poses no problem to almighty God. If God can create a universe out of nothing, and fashion mankind from clay, and sustain the whole race in life, can he not easily reassemble dismantled bodies?

But *after* death and hades have delivered up the dead, what then? The Word tells us, "Death and hades were cast into the lake of fire." They have served their purpose and therewith are destroyed forever. We are also told that the lake of fire is "the second death." What is that "second death"? It is *gehenna,* the final doom of the lost. What, then, is that "lake of fire" which is also the "second death"? Well, remember that we are here dealing with *vision,* not literal definition. That fire will not be physical; but fire is used figuratively to indicate how terrible is that final doom.

Oh, the awfulness of gehenna! Of the twelve times that it is named in the New Testament, eleven times it is Jesus who warns us of it. His warnings are startling in their stark syllables and may well stir us to concern for the Christ-rejecting thousands around us. We would lift up our voice and cry, "Escape the damnation of gehenna where the worm dieth not and the flame is not quenched!"

A FINAL CLARIFICATION

And now, in a final word, let me try to correct what I consider to be a bad misunderstanding about that coming Judgment Day, lest the doctrine of gehenna should seem to cast a libel on the character of God. Reflect: no born-again Christian will stand before that Great White Throne. Scripture makes that crystal-clear. "He that believeth . . . hath everlasting life, and shall *not* come into judgment" (John 5:24). Therefore, all those who stand before that dread judgment-seat will be *non-Christians.* Yes, indeed, but do they all, without exception, go to gehenna? Let him prove it who can.

Mark carefully. What happens at that vast assize is not an indiscriminate, wholesale consignment of all that multi million multitude to gehenna. If that is what God has in mind, why any need for a Judgment Day at all? That is not the God of the Bible. The coming Judgment Day will be a *real* judgment; a judicial arraignment before him who is the infallibly omniscient and inflexibly righteous Judge. Cases will be tried. Evidence will be weighed. Verdicts will be reached. Sentences will be passed. Destinies will be decided. It will be no long-dragging judicial process such as often wearies litigants in earthly law courts, for the divine Judge is infinite, with a knowledge that is absolute and immediate; also, time will then have become timelessness.

Twice in that Scripture passage describing the Judgment Day, we read: "They were judged, every man, *according to their works.*" So no man will be damned because of *Adam's* sin, or for being a member of Adam's fallen race. Every man will be judged according to the light he had and the way he lived of his own free will.

See now the final, solemn outcome. The Word says, "And whosoever was not found written in the book of life was cast into the lake of fire." We may well shudder and wish that those words were not there: but they *are* there. What is the Book of Life? It is the book of *all* human life from beginning to end of human history. It is not the book of *only* the redeemed in Christ, as most of us have been taught. No, according to its name, it is the book of *all* human life. Every human being has an original entry; but there are those whose names are "blotted out" through wickedness, impenitence, unbelief and Christ-rejection.

Observe carefully: *not all* in that vast non-Christian multitude are relegated to that lake of fire; for the Word says that only those go there whose names are no longer in the Book of Life. A common teaching by ardent evangelicals is that *all* who stand before that Great White Throne will be damned forever in gehenna; but that is wrong, for it flies in the face of what Scripture actually says. As a matter of exactness, although the King James Version reads, "Whosoever was not found written in the book of life was cast into the lake of fire," a truer rendering of the Greek is, "And *if anyone* was not found written . . ." So not all go to that lake of fire; but some do. Gehenna is the extreme penalty, but it is not the *only* penalty. As there are degrees of reward for faithful service, so there *must* be degrees of punishment for degrees of guilt. Will God treat a noble Socrates or many an upright mother and a blaspheming mass-murderer like Stalin or Hitler without making any distinction? Nay, "Shall not the Judge of all the earth do right?" (Gen. 18:25). Will God recognize no difference between the innocent who never heard the name of Jesus while they were on earth and those who both knew the Gospel and spurned it? Of course he will.

That being so, what happens to those in that vast crowd who escape gehenna? Are they "saved"? No, not in the sense that Christians are; for although they escape gehenna they do not escape the righteous judgment of God. *All* sin will be punished, and as Hebrews 10:31 says, "It is a fearful thing to fall into the hands of the living God." But if they are not saved in the sense that we Christians are, and yet do not go to gehenna, what will their destiny be? I do not know. Where the Bible is silent, I will not presume to speculate. They are not "born again." They can never be in that elect communion of souls which the New Testament calls "the Church," the mystic body and bride and temple of God's dear Son; nor can they share that highest heaven which the glorified saints share with Christ. Let no careless thinking deceive anyone. What we have just said does not give anybody a so-called "second chance." There is *no* second chance to escape that awesome judgment throne; nor is there any certainty apart from Christ that the "second death" or "lake of fire" can be escaped. That is in God's hands, not yours or mine.

But most awesome and frightening of all is that there are some human beings who, before ever they stand at that dread throne, are condemned already to gehenna. Who are they? They are those who are *unbelievers,* Christ-rejectors. Listen again to John 3:18, "He that believeth not is condemned [judged] already, because he hath not believed in the name of the only begotten Son of God." Such deliberate Christ-rejectors are not just neutral *non*believers; they are by free choice *un*believers. Far better that a man live and die as a benighted idolater, never having heard the Gospel, than that he should have known it and rejected it. That is the damning sin; not the breaking of Moses' law, but "doing despite" to the redeeming love of God, and trampling underfoot the blood of the divine Savior. There is no hope for such deliberate ingrates. It is they themselves who blot out their names from the Book of Life and seal their own perdition in gehenna.

Fearful thought! I tremble to think of it, and would cry to every unbeliever, "Stop, listen, reconsider. Make haste to receive the dear Savior while opportunity tremulously lingers. Have done with perilous procrastination. More souls will go to the lake of fire through procrastination than human arithmetic can calculate. Now is the time to act. Death has a way of striking unexpectedly. Then the last chance is gone. As the tree falls so it lies. There is no coming back, and no 'second chance.' "

If you know and possess the risen Savior, weep tears of gratitude and joy: you are *saved forever;* but if you are knowingly excluding that dear Savior from your life, you are hugging your own perdition. Be warned! We are not just playing on anyone's emotions. We are addressing intelligence, conscience, free will. Let your heart's door be flung open to the risen and living Savior *now*. To possess him is to be eternally *saved*.

THREE

OUR DEPARTED CHRISTIAN LOVED ONES

At several points in these reflections on our departed Christian loved ones, questions may be prompted such as: What about the soul-sleep theory? What about purgatory? What about sheol? In order not to interrupt the continuity of this present study, we postpone dealing with those questions until our next chapters, in which we single them out for separate consideration.

J. S. B.

My purpose here is to have an open-hearted talk with you about our Christian loved ones who have passed from us into the Beyond. Most of us have some tender link or other with that unseen realm; and all of us, as we come to life's later years, find that those links increase, while the ties of earth grow fewer or weaker.

Nothing is more understandable than that our thoughts should turn again and again to those who have been called yonder, and that we should find ourselves asking: Where are they? What of their present state? Our enquiry at the moment is not concerning the departed in general. We are asking about those who, while they were on earth, trusted and loved the Savior, and who, as the Scripture sympathetically puts it, have "fallen asleep" in Jesus. Where are *they*? What is *their* present state? Do they remember us and think of us? Do they still see us, hear us, know us? If they *do* see and hear and know us, are they saddened by the troubles which they see overtaking us on earth? Are they with other Christian loved ones? And if so, do they know each other? Do they actually behold the Savior's face? Are they inactively at rest? or are they actively engaged in beautiful ministries?

It will mean much to us if we hold true and clear views as to what the New Testament teaches on this tender subject. So let me here relate to it in a threefold way: first negatively, second positively, third inferentially.

NEGATIVELY

First, then, *negatively:* we need to clear the ground by making certain facts clear as to where and in what condition our departed Christian loved ones are *not* at present. If we keep close to the New Testament we shall not be deceived by such aberrant theories as that of a supposed purgatory, or by the fatuous guesses of modern spiritism. Nor shall we seek false comfort in the unfounded imaginings and sentimental errors found all too often among professing Christians in our orthodox Protestant denominations.

NOT YET THE CELESTIAL CITY

To begin with, we must not confuse the present state of our departed Christian loved ones with that which is to be theirs after the second coming of Christ. We speak and sing of the pearly gates, the golden street, the jasper walls, and we like to imagine those as being descriptive of the heaven to which our departed Christian loved ones have gone. But where do those ideas about the pearly gates and golden street and jasper walls come from? They are from the last two chapters of the Bible, namely, the Book of the Revelation, chapters 21 and 22. Yet those two chapters do not describe heaven, as is generally supposed; they refer to a resplendent city of the future which is yet to be set up on this earth.

The very first verse of John's photographic description should put us wise to that. He says, "And I John saw the holy city, new Jerusalem, coming *down* from God out of heaven, prepared as a bride adorned for her husband. And I heard a great voice out of heaven saying, Behold, the tabernacle of God is *with men,* and he will dwell with them." We have the same in verse 10, which says that the New Jerusalem *descends* from heaven to earth. Later we are told that the "nations" on *earth* shall "walk in the light" of that city. There are other clear indications that the city is to be on this earth. Therefore that future city must not be equated with heaven. No, it comes *down* from heaven, which means that it is not identical with heaven.

In the Scripture preview of the future, there are four outstanding developments predicted, around which all others gather. Those four are: (1) the return of Christ and the catastrophic ending of the present age at Armageddon; (2) the thousand-year messianic rule of Christ on earth; (3) the final, general judgment of the human race at the Great White Throne; and (4) the dissolution of the present cosmic system and the bringing in of a "new heaven and a new earth."

During the coming Millennium, or thousand-year reign of Christ on earth, the *old* Jerusalem will be rebuilt, but *after* that, and after the final judgment of the race and the bringing in of the "new heaven and earth," the "*new* Jerusalem" will come *down.* When at last that queen city of those yet-future golden ages is planted on earth, all our departed Christian loved ones will have their part in it; but they are *not there now.* That city is not heaven. It is yet future. It will be on earth.

NOT YET THE FINAL REWARD

Further, we must not think of our departed Christian loved ones as having gone to their *final reward.* The New Testament does not teach so. The apostle Paul did not expect to go to his final reward at death even though his death was a martyrdom. This is what he says in 2 Timothy 4:8: "Henceforth there is laid up for me a crown of righteousness, which the Lord, the righteous judge, shall give me at *that day."* What does Paul mean by "that day"? The context makes the answer clear. The chapter begins: "I charge thee therefore before God, and the Lord Jesus Christ, who shall judge the quick and the dead at his *appearing and his kingdom."* So in this paragraph Paul's eye is on our Lord's second advent. When he here speaks about "that day" he means the future return and kingdom of Christ. And it is to *then* that he looks for his crowning reward. That is made finally certain by the latter part of verse 8, "Henceforth there is laid up for me a crown of righteousness which the Lord, the righteous Judge, shall give me at that day: and not to me only, but unto all them also that love *his appearing."*

Other passages might be cited to the same effect. Not only Paul, but all other Christian believers receive their final reward at "that day." Peter and John concur with Paul. (See 1 Peter 5:1-4, and 1 John 3:1-2.) Let us understand clearly therefore: the Christian's final reward is linked with that yet-future return of our royal Savior, and with our resurrection-translation into his likeness, and our sharing in his earth-girdling kingdom. Therefore, our departed Christian loved ones cannot yet have gone to their final reward.

NOT YET IN GLORIFIED BODIES

Again, we must not think of our departed Christian loved ones as possessing *glorified bodies* such as are promised to our Lord's people at the coming resurrection. When he returns in second-advent splendor there will be an unimaginably wonderful resurrection in which the bodies of all born-again Christians who have passed through death will be restored to them. Not that those resurrection bodies will be identical in substance with those which were laid in the grave or were otherwise disintegrated. Our resurrection bodies will have a real relation and likeness to the body which was laid aside at death, but they will be indescribably superior. They will be similar in *structure* but different in *texture.* They will be supernal and immortal bodies.

Possessing glorified bodies will be surpassingly wonderful when it happens, but it has not happened yet; and until it happens our departed Christian loved ones do *not* possess their promised resurrection-bodies of deathless beauty. We must not think of them as being either in those yet-future bodies or as possessing, in some intermediate shadowy form, the bodies which were laid in the grave or cremated or otherwise dissolved. Strange as it seems to some of us, there are those who teach that Christian believers are clad in their resurrection bodies immediately after death. Only recently I read a scholarly book by an eminent Scottish theologian which propounds that idea. We need not branch aside to discuss that view now. Let it be bypassed until a later chapter, where it will be given consideration. All I would say here, with cordial respect to those who hold that theory, is that I cannot find a single verse in the New Testament where it is either stated or implied. As Paul states in Romans 8:23, the "redemption of our *body,*" although included in the salvation wrought for us by our Lord's atoning death, has not yet been effected in actual experience, nor will it be until our Lord's return. In that verse Paul says that although we Christians already have "the firstfruits of the Spirit," we "groan within ourselves, *waiting* . . . for the redemption of the *body.*"

So then, to sum up our negative precautions: we must not confuse the present *intermediate* state of our departed Christian loved ones with their yet-future *ultimate* state after the second coming of Christ: (1) They have not yet gone to the city of pearly gates; (2) they have not yet received their final reward for service; and (3) they are not yet clothed with their resurrection bodies.

POSITIVELY

Having now made those negative aspects clear, let us answer *positively,* keeping closely in step with New Testament statements.

WITH CHRIST

The first big, positive fact which stands out is that our departed Christian loved ones are *with Christ*. We do not need to hunt for passages where this may be implied or inferred. We have it in plain statement. Let me read just two verses which, if we honestly and naturally interpret them, i.e., without manipulating them to fit prefabricated theories, most definitely teach that our Christian departed are now with Christ.

The first text is 2 Corinthians 5:8. Paul says, "We are confident, I say, and willing rather to be absent from the body, and to be present *in purgatory.*" I beg your pardon. I have misquoted the text. Let me read it again. "We are willing rather to be absent from the body and to be in a coma of *soul-sleep.*" I must beg your pardon again. That is neither the Authorized nor the Revised Version; it is the *de*vised version, and it is wrong.

Please do not charge me with irreverence or facetiousness. I have read what the text does *not* say in order to emphasize what it *does* say. Let me now read the actual words. "We are confident, I say, and willing to be absent from the body, and to be present *with the Lord.*" Observe: there are just the two alternatives: (1) in the body, absent from the Lord; and (2) absent from the body, present with the Lord.

That is made the more definite when we consult the context. In the earlier verses, Paul speaks of our being eventually clothed with the resurrection body, which he calls "a house not made with hands, eternal in the heavens." Then he refers to an intermediate state in which we are no longer in this mortal body but have not yet been "clothed upon" with that "house" which is to be ours at the second coming of Christ. Notice, he does not say that to be absent from *this* body is to be clothed with *that* body; but he does say that to be absent from this body is to be "present with the Lord." Clearly, there is an intermediate state during which we are temporarily bodiless; but nowhere in Scripture is there any allusion to an intermediate *body*. Nor are we told the *mode* of life which disembodied Christians now live. That, however, only serves to make more conspicuous this first big fact, that Christians who have crossed to the other side of death are "with Christ."

The other text I refer to is Philippians 1:23-24. Paul says, "I am in a strait betwixt two, having a desire to depart, and to be *in purgatory*." Forgive me, wrong again! I purposely misquoted Paul's words so as to emphasize again what is *not* said. Look at the words again: "I am in a strait betwixt two, having a desire to depart and to drop into a complete blackout of soul-sleep." Nothing of the kind! That again is what the text does *not* say. With alert mind, observe what Paul actually *does* say. "I am in a strait betwixt two, having a desire to depart and to be *with Christ;* which is far better."

The context clearly establishes that when the apostle thus spoke of departing to be with Christ he did *not* mean departing to be with him by-and-by in the yet future resurrection body. He meant being with him immediately upon vacating the present mortal body. His very next comment (v. 24) surely settles that; for he adds, "Nevertheless to abide in the flesh [ministering among you] is more needful for you." So, there were just the two alternatives in his mind—either departing and being with Christ, or abiding here in the body a while longer.

Now I know that there is a remarkable kind of so-called Bible teaching which by exegetical jugglery and expository gymnastics can so manipulate a text as to make it mean practically the opposite of what it actually says. We marvel at the cleverness of it but deplore the causistry of it. Peter calls it "wresting" the Scriptures. With simple, honest conviction I maintain that if we read the aforementioned two texts in the way they were evidently *meant* to be taken, there cannot be a shadow of doubt about it, that at the death of the body the disembodied Christian believer is immediately "with Christ."

WITH CHRIST CONSCIOUSLY

But now, the second big fact pertaining to our departed Christian loved ones is that they are "with Christ" *consciously*. There is a theory known as the "soul-sleep" theory, which says that at the death of the body the disembodied soul of the Christian becomes unconscious and remains so until the second advent of Christ. I ask you to reject that notion as being untrue to the full biblical data. Those who hold it and teach it do so by overstraining a certain few texts away back in Job, the Psalms, and Ecclesiastes, and then overturning the meaning of others. Do I need to remind you that the Bible is a *developing* revelation, reaching its clearest and fullest teachings in the *New* Testament? For Christians, the final word is in the New Testament. Therefore, to let a few doubtful Old Testament references to the grave blur the mind to all the fuller revelation in the New Testament seems to me a strange behavior.

It would mean too long a diversion to discuss the soul-sleep theory here. Let a consideration of it be postponed until a later chapter. For the moment I refer to just one text which, it seems to me, is quite incompatible with the soul-sleep idea. That text is Philippians 1:21, where Paul's exulting word is, "For to me to live is Christ, and to die is gain." Would Paul ever have said, "to die is gain," if from the moment of his demise he was to lie in the stark oblivion of soul-sleep for an indeterminate duration? What possible "gain" could it have been, to leave his Spirit-filled ministry, his rich communion with Christ, his bringing of thousands to know the Savior, his founding of churches around the world, his teaching of believers, his inspired letter-writing for the guidance and edification of the Christian assemblies? As 2 Corinthians 12:1-4 tells us, Paul had been "caught up" by the Holy Spirit and given more than a glimpse of what awaits the Christian on the other side of death; and *that* is what he has in mind when he exults, "To die is *gain*"! When we reflect on Paul's words, and on other New Testament statements which we shall look at in later chapters, we can only be the more confirmed in rejecting the soul-sleep theory. I gladly acknowledge the thorough sincerity of those who teach it. Nonetheless we must reject it as unscriptural and misleading.

WITH CHRIST LOCALLY

And that brings us to a third proposition, namely, that our departed Christian loved ones are not only "with Christ" consciously; they are with him *locally*. The heaven to which they have gone is not only an inward experience or subjective condition of blessedness; it is a *place*. As the sun is everywhere present in our solar system by the light and heat which it diffuses—besides the one place where it concentratedly *is*—so, and much more so, God is everywhere immanent throughout the universe, while yet there is one place, inconceivable as yet to our finite minds, where apparently his throne and presence are ineffably concentrated. That place is heaven in the supreme sense (for Scripture indicates a plurality of "heavens"). It was from there that our Lord came—which is why 1 Corinthians 15:47 calls him "the Lord from *heaven.*" It was to there that he returned after he had completed his atoning work on earth—which is why Mark 16:19 says, "He was received up into *heaven,* and sat on the right hand of God." Note in that latter text: heaven is where the throne or "right hand" of God is.

In that sense, *heaven* (singular) is to be distinguished from *heavens* (plural). Hebrews 4:14 says, "We have a great high priest who is passed *through* the heavens" (plural). But in Hebrews 9:24 we read: "For Christ is . . . entered . . . into heaven *itself* [emphatic singular], now to appear in the *presence of God* for us." Observe that "heaven itself" is intensively the "presence of God."

Think what that means in relation to our departed Christian loved ones. Our divine Savior, as God the Son, is omnipresent, but in his now-glorified body and humanhood he is *there,* amid the glory-light of that heaven, in a peculiarly manifest way. And if *he* is there, so are our dear departed; for 2 Corinthians 5:8 says (let us gratefully repeat it), "To be absent from the body" is to be "present [or at home] with the Lord"! Was that the place to which Paul referred when he spoke of having been caught up to the "third heaven" or "paradise," where he had experienced such a foretaste of rapture as could not be divulged on earth? It would seem so. If the "third heaven" or "paradise" is not identical with that supreme heaven, it is certainly in close association with it.

That being so, think what the bliss of our dear ones must be yonder. Although, as yet, they are not "clothed upon" with their promised resurrection bodies, their present state is one of exquisite fellowship with Christ; of ineffable felicity and surpassing joy. They know now why Paul wrote, "I have a desire to depart and to be with Christ, which is *far better.*" What rapture indeed, to be in that dear Savior's unclouded presence! As Mrs. Anne Cousin sings,

> *The King there in his beauty*
> *In shadeless light is seen;*
> *It were a well-spent journey*
> *Tho' seven deaths lay between.*

Imagine, if you can, what it must be to live in a state of such inwrought holiness that no selfish thought, no unkind or impure motive, no wrong desire, ever clouds the mind; where no anxiety ever disturbs one's deep heart-rest; where no temptation ever shoots its gilded but poisoned arrows; where no suffering or sorrow ever rends one's spirit; and where no jarring discord of any kind ever sounds amid the deep, rich harmonies of a sinless society. That is where our departed Christian loved ones are. Not only are they themselves in heaven; they have heaven in themselves.

Would you catch one flashing glimpse of that fair realm and of our Christian kindred there? Turn to the last book of Holy Writ: Revelation 7:9-17. In that passage John sees a "great multitude, which no man could number, of all nations, and kindreds, and peoples, and tongues," standing before the throne of God and before the Lamb, "clothed with white robes" and having palm branches (symbol of victory) in their hands. A heavenly interpreter explains to John the meaning of the vision. "These are they which came out of great tribulation, and have washed their robes, and made them white in the blood of the Lamb."

The usual teaching is that those countless thousands with their white robes and victory-palms are those who will be saved during the three-and-a-half-year "great tribulation" expected at the end of the present age. I have a growing persuasion, however, that the usual teachings about that supposedly age-end "great tribulation" may need revising. Some of the ideas floating round are certainly not quite scriptural. But in any case, if we translate the Greek exactly, the verse should read, "These are they who are *coming* out of great tribulation." That Greek participle, *"coming,"* indicates a *continuous* coming rather than an all-in-one event. What happens at the end of this present age may well be a climax, but the coming of Christians out of "great tribulation" has been going on all through the Anno Domini centuries, from the prodigal anti-Christian atrocities of that royal maniac, Nero, right down to the present-day concentration camps of Soviet Russia.

No wonder they are a "multitude which no man could number." John sees them and records the vision of them in that seventh chapter of the Apocalypse:

> Therefore are they before the throne of God, and serve him day and night in his temple: and he that sitteth on the throne shall dwell among them. They shall hunger no more, neither thirst any more; neither shall the sun light on them, nor any heat. For the Lamb which is in the midst of the throne shall feed them, and shall lead them unto living fountains of waters: and God shall wipe away all tears from their eyes. (vs. 15-17)

Oh, think of it again: that vision is something which is having a continuous fulfillment *now!* Even the vision of it which was given to John cannot adequately vivify it to us while we are here in these mortal bodies, limited to our physical senses, and incapable of realizing what it must be to dwell in that non-physical realm of rapture. It is blessedness beyond all present imagination. But they are *there.* The saved ones whom we have known and loved on earth are *there,* in that fair realm of sublime fulfillments and unfading joys. As we think of them there, dare we ever wish them back here?

INFERENTIALLY

But now, thirdly and finally, following upon our three negatives and three positives, may we not draw certain very comforting inferences, still keeping close to the New Testament? I think we may; but let me make clear that in this final section of our reflections on this tender subject I speak with no dogmatism. I shall try not to infer *too* much from any given text, but I shall gratefully appropriate what I think is really warranted.

First, then, I believe that our departed Christian loved ones *see us, know us, and pray for us.* Hebrews 12:1 says, "Wherefore seeing we also are compassed about with so great a cloud of *witnesses,* let us . . . run with patience the race that is set before us." Who are those "witnesses" who encompass us? Some expositors reply that they are those Old Testament heroes of faith who fill the preceding chapter. Those old-time worthies, so some say, are not witnesses in the sense that they now watch us from the other side of the grave, but only in the sense that they were "witnesses" for God in the long-ago when they lived on earth. But does that explanation do justice to the text? The Greek verb which our King James Version translates as "compassed about" is a present-tense participle, and the line in which

56

it occurs should read, "With all this host of witnesses *now encircling us.*" I think that to be really fair to the passage, we must believe that those invisible spectators are said to be watching us *now.* If, then, *they* observe us, are our departed Christian loved ones *debarred* from doing so? Is not a reasonable presumption that they too see us, watch us, and know what is happening to us?

Be reminded again of our Lord's words about the "rich man" and Lazarus (Luke 16). After his death, the rich man, disembodied and pauperized, found himself in hades; and there he pleaded for his five brothers who were still on earth. If the departed in hades thus think of those still on earth, do not our departed Christian dear ones in heaven still think of *us,* and similarly pray for us?

When Moses and Elijah appeared with our Lord Jesus on the Mount of Transfiguration, it soon became evident that *they* had been watching developments on earth and were able to talk familiarly about them. Is not the same inferable of Christians who are now yonder? Though they are lost to *our* sight, are we lost to *theirs?*

I cannot help remembering Paul's words in 1 Corinthians 4:9. Let me read it as it is translated in the New International Version:

> For it seems to me that God has put us apostles on display at the end of the procession, like men condemned to die in the arena. We have been made a *spectacle* to the whole universe, to angels as well as to men.

That word *spectacle* in the Greek is *theatron,* a place for public shows, a theater for the performance of drama before spectators. It is an arresting figure. Perhaps the common saying, "All the world's a stage," is truer than many think. Paul says that he and his fellow-apostles were like actors on a theater stage, and the spectators were not only men here on earth, but angels and other realms. That is hardly an exaggeration of the apostle's meaning, nor, as we ponder it carefully, need it be too surprising; for God has revealed himself on this planet, and unveiled a divine drama of redeeming love, beyond all he has ever shown or done on any other habitable globe. The one point I stress here is that if angels and others in those non-earthly spheres are witnesses of what goes on here, are not our departed Christian loved ones observers also?

Remember: there is no geography in the spirit-realm. There is no such barrier as distance—not in the way it applies to our physical world and our mortal bodies. How long did it take Moses and Elijah to travel from wherever they were in the unseen realm to join our Lord on that mountain summit? Perhaps the heaven, or the part of it, where our translated Christian brethren are is not as far from this planet as we have traditionally assumed. I think it should be both challenging and comforting to us that those who have gone *there* still see us who are left *here*.

Mind you, I have no scriptural warrant to say that they are near us *continually*. Like all other created beings, they are finite and therefore can be in only one place at any given instant. If they are *there,* in that heavenly paradise, they cannot be simultaneously *here* in the vicinity of earth. Nevertheless, there certainly is *movement* to and from in that spirit-realm. Scripture makes repeatedly clear that the sinless *angels* have often come from there to here with communications for men. May it not be, also, that the indefinable sphere of holy rest where the departed saints are reaches nearer to this old earth (as before suggested) than we have hitherto thought? I speak with no dogmatism, but I think that what we are inferring is a precious likelihood.

WHAT IF THEY SEE US SUFFER?
Someone is sure to ask: Would it not spoil the bliss of heaven for them if they saw us amid the troubles which hurt us here on earth? We may answer that question by asking another: Does it spoil heaven for our Lord Jesus as

he sees those troubles which afflict us? Is it not a consolation to us Christians that he *does* see and know and care? The fact is, of course, that the Lord Jesus sees those troubles differently from the way we ourselves do.

How often, when grievous trouble fells us, we gasp, "Why has this come upon me? What have I done to provoke it? What shall I do? How long will it last? What will be the outcome? Why? Why? Why?" Our grief or fear is intensified because, with our limited vision, we see only the earthward side, the bleak *enigma*. Not so our Lord Jesus. He sees it in the context of an educative divine process leading to rich reward. Similarly, our fellow-believers who are now with him yonder see things no longer in *our* short-sighted way, but in larger light and fuller comprehension. They see our earthly troubles as part of the "all things" which "work together" for our eternal good (Rom. 8:28).

Apropos of that, we may well ask: Does the bliss of those now in heaven depend on their having a *cloak* flung between them and realities here on earth? If so, then the bliss of heaven is in part that of increased ignorance, not of larger light. Surely the serenity of that shadowless region springs from illumed apprehension, not from imposed ignorance.

Mark the contrast which Paul makes in 1 Corinthians 13:12 between "now" on earth and "then" in heaven. He says, "For now we see through a glass [mirror], darkly; but then face to face: now I know in part; but then shall I know even as also I am known." The contrast between seeing "through a mirror" obscurely and seeing "face to face" is fascinating. Mirrors in Paul's days were made of metal and were all too often blurry. When he says that we now see through a glass "darkly," the Greek word is *ainigma* from which comes our word *enigma*. The meaning is that here we often see things so indistinctly that they are enigmas, whereas in heaven they see things "face to face," i.e., as they really are. Admittedly, Paul's words envisage what lies in the ultimate future, but they obviously include also the saints now in heaven, where the ultimate is already experienced except for the yet-future resurrection of the body.

Let us therefore grasp this firmly: our Christian relatives and friends now in heaven see our troubles on earth as differently from our earthly obscurity as radiant morn is different from murky dusk. They see our present adversities in true perspective as parts of a process leading to an infinite compensation.

THEY PRAY FOR US

Further, I believe that in the luminous light of heaven *they pray for us*. We evangelical Christians do not believe in "prayers for the dead." We find no warrant for it in Scripture. We are persuaded, nonetheless, that our dear ones on that other side of death pray for *us*. We do not believe in a sacerdotal priesthood, a separate priest class such as that in the Roman Catholic church; for neither is there any warrant for *that* in the New Testament. The old Aaronic priesthood was done away in Christ, and there certainly is no other separate priest-class taught in the New Testament. The apostles were not priests. They never claimed to be. Nor did they ever appoint priests. Nor did they ever teach any such specialized priesthood. We therefore reject the idea of a separate priest-class as unscriptural. But just as definitely we *do* believe in the priesthood of *all* born-again Christians. Speaking of *all* Christian believers, Peter says in his first epistle, chapter 2:5, "Ye . . . are . . . an holy priesthood." And just afterwards he adds, "Ye are a chosen generation, a royal priesthood."

Yes, all true Christians are priests in Christ. As such they have ever-open access to the throne of God "in his name." Does the believer's priesthood terminate at the grave? Nay, contrariwise, it then enters on its higher exercise. Did our Lord's priesthood end at his death? No, it was then that it *began*. While on earth he was *not* a priest, for he was not of the tribe of Levi. But after making atonement for us by

60

his once-for-all sacrifice of himself he ascended to heaven as our "Great High Priest" forever, "after the order of Melchisedek." What, then, does his high-priesthood there mean to his people still on earth? One of its main aspects is given in Hebrews 7:25: "Wherefore he is able also to save them to the uttermost that come unto God by him, seeing he ever liveth *to make intercession* for them."

Beyond the clouds that drape the sky,
Amid that sinless realm on high,
There gleams a heavenly temple fair,
And Jesus our High Priest is there.

Yes, there for us He intercedes,
And all his Calvary merit pleads,
And represents before the throne
Our needs as if they were his own.

No other priest in heaven I need,
No other priest on earth to plead;
His wounded hands and feet and side
Exclude all need of priests beside.

Along with him, yonder, all his people who have joined him there are exercising *their* now-elevated priesthood as his privileged cointercessors, interceding for us who are still on earth. With far superior intelligence and mental illumination than they had while in the flesh, they continually intercede for you and me during our pilgrimage from here to there. Did you hear that, you who have been bereaved of dear ones and have wondered why God took them? Your treasured one yonder is thinking of you, loving you, *praying* for you; praying for you continually with such enlightened understanding that every such intercession is answered with a divine "Yes," and registers itself in sustenance and blessing which come to you daily. When the final consummation breaks upon us we shall find that their prayers in heaven on our behalf have brought far more blessing to us than if they had lingered longer on earth.

Incidentally, what we are here saying may explain why deaths are permitted which seem inexplicable to us. What we have mistaken for strange unkindness on God's part may have been designed for our lasting blessing by a wisdom which never errs.

ABOUT MARRIAGE UNIONS

I gratefully believe that unions of love made here on earth will *continue* in the Beyond. Someone is sure to remind me of our Lord's words that in the heavenly realm "they neither marry, nor are given in marriage" (Matt. 22:30). Let those words inform us, however, that sex is not indispensable to true love. Here on earth marital love may find its most sacred and intimate expression in what is called "sex," yet sex is not the noblest or most satisfying interchange of heart-to-heart love. The richest experience of love is supra-sex.

Years ago, when I was pianist for the National Young Life Campaign in Britain, we had some crowded meetings in Belfast, Northern Ireland. I stayed there with a dear old couple who had been married over fifty years. He was in his early eighties, and she in her late seventies. With a young man's curiosity (of which I am now ashamed) I asked them, "In your old age do you find your marriage joy as sweet and satisfying as when you were young, ardent, amorous?" Much as I could now blush at my youthful imprudence, I am always grateful for the reply they gave. I can just see the two of them. He, a handsome old gentleman, and she a mild-featured matron with silvered hair and glowing face. They looked into each other's eyes—oh, such a look. Then, taking her into his arms and looking tenderly—oh, so tenderly, into her upraised face he said, "My precious darling, when we went to the marriage altar fifty years ago we thought we loved each other *then,* and we certainly did; but oh, what was that compared with this?" And, momentarily oblivious of my presence, they held each other in an affectionate embrace lovelier than I have ever seen among the young. As I stood there I could not help musing, "What an eye-opener! Sex dead, but love more alive, more personal, more satisfying, yes, more truly *thrilling* than ever!"

In the life beyond, and most of all in that ultimate state of glory after the resurrection of the saints, we shall have senses and powers and attributes and capacities which will provide such expression for love as will make sex crude by comparison.

There is a familiar saying, "Marriages are made in heaven." I believe that many of them *are,* among God's devout minority; but as for others, far too many of them are *not,* for they are made with little or no thought of God, and are wholly of "the flesh." Heart-to-heart unions of Christian lovers will not end with the last heartbeat. Such true love-unions "in the Lord" will go on and on in the Beyond. Whatever different quality of life may be ours hereafter, this much is sure for the Christian: heaven will perfect and perpetuate all that earth has made sacredly dear. Although earthly *family* relationships will be superseded, my dear mother will always be the same person. I myself will always be the *same person.* For the Christian, death neither obliterates human identity nor submerges the individual distinctives of human personality. Those traits and characteristics which are individually peculiar to you and me will not only reappear yonder but will be refined and accentuated. All the unlovely will have been eliminated, and every lovable feature will be retained, emphasized, sublimated. As there have been special loves here, so will there continue to be in that higher life. There will be no problem there pertaining to those who have married more than once while on earth. Where human love is lifted completely above sex, all such supposed problems will evaporate and vanish. Although that may not be explicitly stated in Scripture, it seems implied in such texts as Matthew 22:30 and Luke 20:35-36, where our Lord says that the true "children of the resurrection" are like the unfallen angels, in whom there is a love and joy lifting them above all the merely sensory.

WHAT OF BABES AND INFANTS?

What about those who die as babes or infants? Let me speak with tenderness about that; for what I say may possibly come to parents who have been recently bereaved of a little one. Dear father, mother, have no doubt about this: your precious bairn is safely yonder, in a better home than any on earth, and in a fair clime where none of earth's hurts ever come to the little folk.

Realize this, also, that your cherished child will "grow up" there, just as would have happened on earth if the dear little soul had stayed here with you. Never think of your child there as *static*. There are no such abnormalities as immortal babies. There is no such thing as everlasting childhood. You would not wish it so, would you? If we think logically about it, instead of allowing wistful sentiment to take over, we simply must realize (thankfully so) that in heaven there is no perpetual suspension of growth, no permanent immaturity. All is progressive vitality. As for our departed little ones, it is development from infancy to unsullied maturity and fleckless beauty. Perhaps we can all sympathize with the parental sentiment in the following lines:

> *Two little feet went pattering by,*
> *Years ago;*
> *They wandered off to the sunny sky*
> *Years ago:*
> *They nestle no more in the arms they left,*
> *They never came back to the home bereft*
> *Years ago.*
>
> *But again I'll hear those two little feet*
> *Pattering by;*
> *Their music a thousand times more sweet*
> *Up in the sky:*

I know that in God the Father's care
My babe is safe till we meet up there,
  By and by.

Such sentiment tugs at one's heartstrings, but it does not correspond with reality. Thank God, in this instance the reality is better than the sentiment. It is natural, of course, that mothers and fathers should picture their lost little ones as infants. Who does not love to see a dear little wondering-eyed baby around the house? But why should parents want to meet their fondly loved offspring still as babes years ahead? If they *did* find them so after all the intervening time-lapse, there would be grief instead of joy. Make no mistake, the Bible indicates something far better: a reassuring hope which kisses parental tears into jewels of valid anticipation. Should it not thrill any mother to know that the darling treasure taken from her bosom as a tiny infant will be seen again, not as an unopened bud, but as a full-bloomed rose in the garden of paradise?

I am not fancifully romancing when I say that in heaven there are wonderful nurseries where angels and other gentle-hearted guardians bring up the little ones through kindergarten to youth and adulthood. Dear parent, if your child had remained on earth there would have been a *pari passu* development of mind and body. There is a corresponding development in heaven *apart* from the body until the resurrection day. In an environ where there is no temptation, no sin, no guile, no shadow, no infantile sickness, no fear or crying, your little one is growing to such eventual stature and immaculate beauty that when at last you meet again on that resurrection morn, you will exclaim, "God has done all things well! I would not have had it otherwise. How wonderful to see my little one grown to such loveliness and trained for such sacred ministries!" What a reunion that will be!

WHAT THEN ABOUT DYING?

And now, to finalize these reflections about our departed Christian loved ones, it is pertinent to ask: What should our thoughts and feelings be about *dying?* To the young, life on earth seems long in prospect; but we who have left youth behind and have traveled on to our elder years realize how short life on earth is. Soon enough all of us must pass over to that other side of the grave. What, then, about dying? That is no morbid question. It is just as rational as it is eventually inescapable.

There certainly is no morbidity about it so far as we *Christians* are concerned. For all of us who know the Lord Jesus as our Savior, the grave has been transformed from a foe to a friend. What is called "death" has become the gate to immortal consummation in the palace of our heavenly King. We may well feel concern, indeed we *do* feel acute concern, for those who go through this earthly span with their hearts deliberately closed to that one-and-only Savior. To them the death of the body is the gloomy portal to a far deeper gloom beyond. However, we are thinking here particularly of those who know and love the dear Savior, who by simple but vital faith have received him, thereby becoming saved forever.

To all such I say, with the backing of the Bible: *You need have no fear of death.* On the contrary, it will be a wonderful experience. However painful to the flesh it sometimes is for the bird to struggle out of the cage, the actual release to the real *you,* to mind and heart, will be wonderful. Your last breath here will instantaneously give place to deathless life, complete healing, and exquisite joy *there.* The last earthly shadow will melt in the cloudless glory-light of a better world. What we call "the valley of the shadow" here on this side is so bright with light from the *other* side, that as soon as we enter it, darkness vanishes. Underneath and round about us are the "everlasting arms" of the love that never lets us go. We find ourselves looking into the dearest face in the universe. Jesus and heaven are ours! In a word, sunset here is sunrise there!

Years ago, when I lived in Edinburgh, Scotland, some friends of mine told me about an elderly lady who came to the city on business several days each week. She always came by railway train. On the northern side of the city, just before the train reaches Waverley Station, there is a very long tunnel, of which, with its deep darkness, the dear elderly lady was scared. In fact, such was her fear of that long, dark tunnel that she always used to get off of the train at the Haymarket Station, which is the last stop before the train slowly glides through the long darkness into Waverley Station. One day, however, the dear lady was unusually tired, and dozed off to sleep in the train. With a sudden start she woke to find herself actually in the Waverley Station, having peacefully come through that dreaded "long, dark tunnel!" As she rubbed her eyes she gave a little chuckle and rebuked herself, "Why on earth was I ever scared of *that?*"

We may well parallel that with Christian believers in relation to death. Why vex ourselves with fears which are as needless as they are groundless? For Christians, death on its earthward side is simply that the tired mortal body falls temporarily to sleep, while on the heavenward side we suddenly find ourselves with our dear Savior-King and with other Christian loved ones in the heavenly home. Why fear that? Let us go to meet death, singing with Paul, "For to me to live is Christ, *and to die is gain!*"

FOUR

WHAT OF THOSE WHO DIE IN INFANCY?

Mothers sometimes say of their little one, "I wish he would never grow up!" We all understand that little bit of sentimental falsehood. But suppose the little one did *not* grow up. What concern! What sorrow! What anxious pursuit of the best medical assistance! Protracted infancy would be infinitely more tragic in heaven than on earth.

J. C. Macauley

When I was a child, I spake as a child, I understood as a child, I thought as a child: but when I became a man, I put away childish things.

1 Corinthians 13:11

Infancy, in the Bible, always implies immaturity, incompleteness, imperfection.

J. S. B.

The Bible teaches that man was created in innocency and placed in an environ of blemishless congeniality. Because he was a free agent, some kind of probation was necessary. Such probation implied liability to temptation, but there was no reason to yield, and every reason to become established in holiness and undying life. Subsequently man disobeyed, thereby forfeiting innocence and bringing upon his posterity the "curse" of both physical and spiritual death.

That curse, however, was not only a judicial sentence imposed from without; it was a moral *disease* contracted within. Human nature itself became infected, and because the human race is bound together by procreation and heredity, that depravity became transmitted to each new offspring. In that sense, when Adam fell, the unborn generations of his children fell with him.

Thank God, in our Lord Jesus Christ there is the Good News of salvation both from the *penalty* of sin (the judicial aspect) and from the *pollution* of sin (the moral aspect). The Bible tells us that all who become united to him by simple but real faith are eternally saved, and will ultimately be fully restored, even "glorified." It also warns that all who

71

willfully reject the gospel seal their own doom beyond the grave.

That raises an issue not only of singular interest but of solemn concern: *Are those who die as infants saved?* It is a poignant and far-reaching question. Despite the reduction in infant mortality, thanks to increasing hygienic and scientific practices, and despite the large suppression of infanticide in non-Christian lands, even today the world's annual death-roll shows that about one quarter of those who are born on this earth die in immaturity. So, are those who die in babyhood or childhood saved or lost? Can we accept the fearful notion of "infants a span long" crawling amid purgatorial fires? or the hyper-Calvinist idea of a dark limbo where the souls of unbaptized children grope around forever? or the general heathen belief that they are simply obliterated? Our enquiry is sharpened to a keen edge by such dogmas and beliefs. Thank God, with the Bible open before us, we can move beyond futile speculation or unresolvable obscurity. The Bible can guide us to satisfying certitudes concerning those who die in infancy. Let us shape our enquiry into a threefold order.

1. Can we think that they are lost?
2. Are we sure that they are saved?
3. May we know their present state?

CAN WE THINK THAT THEY ARE LOST?

Perhaps some whom we now address are parents who have lost a dear little one. To them the subject will be the more sacred and tender. We hope they will find what we say enlightening and comforting. Should some close reasoning be necessary here and there, stay with us. Read and *re*read what we say. Look up the Scripture references which we give. Not what men say, but what the Bible really teaches is the decisive touchstone.

First, then: can we think that those who die as children

are *lost?* Our reply is a capital NO. The Bible nowhere says or implies that young children who die are lost. We have scanned the pages of both the Old Testament and the New, but nowhere have we found any such doctrine as that of infant damnation, nor have we been able to trace even a covert hint of anything like it. That, I agree, is but a negative argument; but if the Bible is what it claims and proves to be, namely the inspired Word of God, then there is a corresponding significance in what it does *not* teach about certain matters. In this instance the negative is almost as good as a positive. The Bible does *not* teach anywhere that our deceased little ones are lost.

Further, it is unthinkable that such infants should be judged and condemned inasmuch as *they have no personal guilt.* There is nothing they have done on which judgment could be passed, and therefore nothing for which to be condemned.

I was astonished to read in one of the famous C. H. Spurgeon's printed sermons that children have original *guilt.* He says, "Though they have not sinned after the similitude of Adam's transgression, they have original guilt." Spurgeon has always been my preacher-exemplar, but on that point he surely has sadly erred. Hereditary sin-infection in newborn babes is one thing, but guilt is quite another. There is no such thing as inherited *guilt.* Nay, guilt belongs only to those who have themselves broken God's law—which innocent infants have *not* done. Romans 4:15 says, "Where no law is, there is no transgression," and chapter 5:13 adds, "Sin is not imputed where there is no law." Those two statements together mean that where there is no transgression (as in the case of infants) there is no guilt (for guilt is a legal term).

In that fifth chapter of Romans Paul explains that people who lived between Adam and Moses were sinners but not transgressors. That was because, until God gave the Law through Moses, men were not transgressing a God-given command. Yet although they were not "transgressors" (the legal aspect) they nevertheless were "sinners" in their *nature* (the moral aspect). So is it with human babes. Admittedly they do inherit the common sin-infection of fallen human nature, but that does not make them legally *guilty* and liable to penalty. Away with such a thought! The little ones are utterly guiltless, and therefore simply could not be judged or condemned.

We are the more firmly assured that departed infants are not lost when we reflect that *they have never rejected the Savior.* The accepting or rejecting of Christ is the decisive factor in the salvation of the soul. Be a man ever so sinful, if he but truly repents and receives the risen Savior his sins shall be pardoned, his guilt removed, and his ugly stains washed away; for the Gospel promise is, "The blood of Jesus Christ, God's Son, cleanseth us from *every* sin" (1 John 1:7). But on the other hand, be a man ever so moral or religious according to human estimates, if he knowingly rejects the redeeming love of God in Christ, he commits the sin which dwarfs all others; for he has "trodden under foot the Son of God" and has "counted the blood of the covenant . . . an unholy thing" and has "done despite unto the Spirit of grace" (Heb. 10:29). As John 3:18 says, he is "condemned already, because he hath not believed in the name of the only begotten Son of God." If he dies in that condition he goes into eternity in uttermost alienation from God. But as for innocent *infants* whose little bodies the grave has claimed, they certainly have *never rejected Christ,* nor have they ever had even a first chance to *accept* him; so that from either aspect they are utterly *blameless.*

Again, it is unthinkable that they are lost, for they have absolutely none of those *self-acquired characteristics* which call forth the displeasure of God. In Matthew 25 our Lord depicts a scene of future judgment. The millions before that judgment-seat are divided into "sheep" on the right hand and "goats" on the left. The former inherit the "kingdom" prepared for them. The latter go to a punishment "prepared for the devil and his angels." What *causes* their banishment? Our Lord tells them: "I was an hungered, and ye gave me no meat: I was thirsty, and ye gave me no drink: I was a stranger, and ye took me not in: naked, and ye clothed me not: sick, and in prison, and ye visited me not." Observe: it is their *not* having done certain things which constitutes their culpability, because it exposes a wrong attitude to Christ himself.

Is it for one second thinkable that Christ should ever say to little ones who have scarce learned to know their right hand from their left, "I was hungered, and ye gave me no meat," etc.? What an ironic mockery of infantile inability that would be! In any case, their undeveloped little minds would not understand a syllable of it. Neither actively nor passively is there anything in a babe which could call forth judicial sentence. The only place where the "Good Shepherd" could place the "lambs" is among the "sheep."

We may crystallize these reasonings in this proposition: It is incompatible with the righteousness of God that the innocent should perish; therefore, those who die as infants cannot be lost. This is such firm, scriptural ground that one wonders how anybody could think otherwise. Yet Spurgeon, of all people, says:

> Some ground the idea of the eternal blessedness of the infant upon its *innocence*. We do no such thing. We believe that the infant fell in the first Adam "for in Adam all died." All Adam's posterity, whether infant or adult, were represented by him, and when he fell he fell for them all. There was no exception made . . . as to infants dying. . . . They are "born in sin and shaped in iniquity; in sin do their mothers conceive them," so saith David of himself and (by inference) of the whole human race. If infants be saved it is not because of any natural innocence. They enter heaven by the very same way that we do: they are received in the name of Christ.

Spurgeon is wrong. Heaven save us from theological hair-splitting, but accuracy is vital. Let us be precise then:

75

those who die as children are not saved *by* their innocence, but they are saved *because* of it. They are not saved *by* it, for it does not expurgate the hereditary infection: but they are saved *because* of it, inasmuch as the infinite merit of the atonement made by our Lord Jesus covers *all* such innocence. Even Spurgeon has to contradict himself; for a few paragraphs later he says, "I cannot conceive it possible of him as the loving and tender One, that when he shall sit to judge all nations he should put the little ones on the left hand, and banish them forever from his presence." In those further words Spurgeon is really saying, as we ourselves are, that with such a Savior, the utterly innocent simply cannot perish.

Pursuant of that, we refuse to think that departed infants are lost, for it would contradict the *character and attitude of God* as revealed in his Word. We recall texts like Jonah 4:11, "Should not I spare Nineveh, that great city, wherein are more than six score thousand persons that cannot discern between their right hand and their left hand?" Those were the little babies in Nineveh. If God was so solicitous for them physically, does not that argue his far greater concern for them as young souls with a timeless destiny? In Ezekiel 16:21 see God's anger at the idolatrous cruelty to little ones whom He calls "*my* children." Or listen again to Jesus as He says, "Let the little ones come unto me." Always remember: when we read the sayings and doings of Jesus, it is *God* who is speaking and moving before us. When Jesus says, "Let the little ones come to *me*," it is *God's* voice we are hearing, and *God's* heart being expressed. How could we reconcile such a revelation of God with the idea that those who die as children are lost?

There is a remarkable epitaph on a tombstone in St. Andrews, Scotland, attributed to Coleridge.

> *Bold infidelity, turn pale and die,*
> *Beneath this stone four infants' bodies lie.*
> *Say, are they lost or saved?*

76

If death's by sin, they've sinned,
for they are here;
If heaven's by works, in heav'n
they can't appear.
Reason! oh, how depraved!
Turn to the Bible's sacred page,
the knot's untied:
They died, for Adam sinned: they live
for Jesus died.

Last but not least, the idea that infants perish *contradicts the plainest truth of the Gospel*. That Gospel is the "Good News" of divine grace abounding to the worst of sinners. The God of the Gospel is a "God who is rich in mercy"; a "God of all compassion"; a God who forgives sins "according to the riches of his grace"; a God who pardons, on the ground of the Calvary atonement, "all manner of sin and blasphemy"; a God who tells us that "where sin abounded, grace did much more abound."

Shall those who have lived their mature years in vice and wickedness repent and be "saved to the uttermost" through faith in Christ, while yet an infant which never knew a wrong thought is cast into the "outer darkness" forever? Perish the thought! If the multimillions of dear little souls who passed from this earth in babyhood are all "lost," could it possibly be true that "where sin abounded, grace did much more abound"? Nay, as the old hymn puts it, "None are excluded [from salvation and heaven] but those who do themselves exclude." There certainly are no self-excluded bairns! If God, through the lips of Jesus, says it to little ones while they live, then surely he says it when they die—*"Let the little ones come unto me."*

ARE WE SURE THAT THEY ARE SAVED?

But now, taking the positive aspect, we ask: Are we sure that they are *saved*? And our reply is a resounding *yes*.

Others, too, have been similarly convinced, but in some cases their reasons have been the watery sands of human fancy rather than the solid ground of biblical truth.

To begin with, we do *not* believe that those who die in infancy are saved by their having been "baptized" or "christened" or "dedicated." To believe so would imply that all infants who have died without the administration of those ordinances are for that reason *lost*. When we consider what an infinitesimal fraction of the total infant-mortality roll those babes are who have been baptized or christened or dedicated before dying, it would be horrifying if infant salvation were limited to such. One would think that in these days of wider education and skeptical realism such sacerdotal impositions as infant baptism or christening would deceive no one; yet singularly enough, even as I was writing these lines my attention was directed to correspondence in a London daily newspaper in which a participant wrote, "If an unbaptized child is killed it has no chance of going to heaven!" Lord, save us from such monstrosities of narrow ritualism and blind bigotry! They are survivals from the Dark Ages, utterly foreign to the teachings of God's written Word.

Nor do we believe that those who die immaturely are saved because they are all *elect*. I quote Spurgeon again: "On what ground then do we believe the child to be saved? We believe it to be as lost as the rest of mankind and as truly condemned. . . . It is saved because it is *elect*. In the compass of divine election we believe that in the Lamb's Book of Life there shall be found written millions of souls who are only shown on earth and then stretch their wings for heaven." Yet surely that peculiar idea, a universal election of infants, is a strange superfluity. It suggests that the larger number of the elect must consist of those who passed away from this earth in babyhood; for those who die as children in any given generation outnumber the comparatively small percentage of those who become "born again" through conversion to Christ.

For myself, I find it difficult to think that such a preponderance of the elect are those who fall prey to death when life has scarcely dawned, before they can possibly know the "effectual call" of the elect in their hearts. Certainly all the elect are saved; but are all the saved elect? Election is far more than salvation from the damnation of gehenna: it is God's choosing of us to be members of the mystic body and bride and temple of his dear Son—members of the true, spiritual church (the *ecclesia,* or called-out ones). Abraham, Moses, Samuel, David, Elijah, Daniel, and other Old Testament saints are all saved and inheritors of the kingdom which our Lord Jesus will yet set up on earth; but are they also in the *ecclesia?* That is something one may well ponder. I speak with no dogmatism about it; but I am convinced of this, that we tread very thin ice if we try to argue the salvation of deceased babes from a supposedly universal infant-election.

Even stranger ideas on this subject are propounded. I cannot expatiate on them here, but they deserve mention if only to be dismissed. There is John Calvin's idea that infants are saved because of *godly ancestry.* He interprets those words of the second commandment, "showing mercy unto thousands," as meaning God's mercy to thousands of *generations;* from which he deduces, apparently, that infants with godly ancestors, even if only remotely, are saved for that reason. There is also the notion, attributed to John Newton, that a vast number, if not all, of those who die in childhood must be saved because, supposedly, the *kingdom of heaven* largely consists of children! It is a comical deduction from our Savior's words, "Suffer the little children to come unto me . . . for of such is the kingdom of heaven." It confuses that kingdom, which is yet to be set up on earth, with the eternal salvation of the soul. We scarcely need tarry to discuss that here; but I strongly dislike the suggestion that the coming kingdom depends largely for its population upon millions of saved infants.

And just once more: infant salvation has been argued

79

from the vast number of the saved as given in Revelation, chapter 7. That vision of the "multitude which no man could number" is familiar to most of us. Read this quotation about it from a contemporary writer:

> Heaven will not be a narrow world. Its population will not be like a handful gleaned from a vintage . . . but ten thousand times ten thousand. Now where are they to come from? How small a part of the map could be called Christian! Out of that part which could be called Christian how small a portion are true believers! Unless the millennial age should soon come . . . I do not see how it is possible that so vast a number as Revelation 7 reveals could be in heaven except on the supposition that infant souls constitute the great majority.

Such surmises are as needless as they are paltry. Among that vast throng of the glorified in Revelation 7 there is not one infant. All are obviously adults, for they "stand" and wave "palms" of victory, and in mighty concert they ascribe "Salvation to our God who sitteth on the throne, and unto the Lamb."

The fact is, we need no such arguments as the aforementioned. They are reeds which break with little pressure. We are better without them, for they divert our minds from the real to the artificial. If we would know for certain that those who pass over as young children are saved, we need no such scraping for crumbs and fragments. Our dear Lord Jesus himself, the infallible teacher, has made the matter clear and decisive once for all, as we shall now see.

THE KING'S OWN GUARANTEE

There are certain characteristics of the Bible which are so recurrent that one might well call them "laws" of written revelation. There is the law of *first mention,* by which we mean that the first mention of any major subject seems invariably the key to all subsequent references to it. There is also the law of *full mention,* by which we mean that somewhere, usually much later, there is a summary or outstanding passage on each leading theme. We think of such passages as 1 Corinthians 15 on the Resurrection; of John 14–16 on the Holy Spirit as the Comforter; of Isaiah 53 on vicarious atonement; and so on. Now there is a classic "full-mention" passage on *infant salvation* in the light of which all other references are to be interpreted. It is Matthew 18:1-14, and the teacher who there speaks to us is our Lord Jesus himself.

First, in verses one and two, we are told the occasion of our Lord's utterance: "At the same time came the disciples unto Jesus saying, Who is the greatest in the kingdom of heaven? And Jesus called a little child unto him, and set him in the midst of them." With that little child as his text, he then spoke memorable words which with final authority settle this matter of infant salvation. His pronouncement in Matthew 18 moves in a fourfold sequence:

1. The kingdom of heaven as it refers to children (vv. 3-5)
2. A warning against our offending of children (vv. 6-9)
3. A warning against our despising of children (v. 10)
4. The heavenly Father's salvation of children (vv. 11-14).

In each of those four Scripture portions our Lord makes a startling statement. First, in verses 3 to 5, he speaks of the *kingdom of heaven* in relation to children:

> Verily I say unto you, Except ye be converted, and become as little children, ye shall not enter into the kingdom of heaven. Whosoever therefore shall humble himself as this little child, the same is greatest in the kingdom of heaven. And whoso shall receive one such little child in my name receiveth me.

The startling feature is that an entrance into the kingdom of heaven requires conversion to childlikeness. There is a wide difference, of course, between being childlike and being *childish.* We certainly are not meant to be childish in mind, but we *are* meant to be child*like* in disposition, with emphasis on childlike humility, simplicity, trustfulness. The implication is that young children already possess that essential passport into the kingdom. No doubt that is why our Lord later added, "For of such is the kingdom of heaven" (Matt. 19:14). If young children possess that first qualification, and the kingdom is said to be "of such," it is utterly unthinkable that "one such little child" could ever be found in that "outer darkness" where there is "weeping and gnashing of teeth."

Look at the second part of our Lord's pronouncement. In Matthew 18:6-9 he warns us against *offending* little children.

> But whoso shall offend one of these little ones which believe in me, it were better for him that a millstone were hanged about his neck, and that he were drowned in the depth of the sea. Woe unto the world because of [such] offences! for it must needs be that offences come; but woe to that man by whom the offence cometh! Wherefore if thy hand or thy foot offend thee, cut them off, and cast them from thee: it is better for thee to enter into life halt or maimed, rather than having two hands or two feet to be cast into everlasting fire. And if thine eye offend thee, pluck it out, and cast it from thee: it is better for thee to enter into life with one eye, rather than having two eyes to be cast into hell [gehenna] fire.

Whatever wider application those words about "offences" have, their first reference is to offences against children. It was our Lord's allusion to the humility and trustfulness of childhood which occasioned them. The very solemnity of the warning to adults measures the preciousness of children to God. And what *kind* of offences against children did Jesus have in mind? He meant hurting them morally and spiritually, for he says, "Whoso shall offend one of these little ones which *believe in me . . .*" Those words cast a lovely flashlight on child conversion. John 2:25 says that our Lord "needed not that any should testify of man: for he knew what was in man." God also knows what is in boys and girls, and that there are many who with beautiful simplicity truly believe on him.

Yes, there are real believers among the young. What their faith lacks in maturity it makes up for in its guileless simplicity. I recall with what vividness I myself believed on Jesus when I was only four, and how I asked that I might pray at the bedside of a sick old lady. Often in later years I have wished that I had never allowed the world to come between Jesus and me. Often have I wished I could regain the simple trust in him which I had then. That trust of child-believers is no mere gullibility; it is native intuition responding to clear teaching breathed upon by the Holy Spirit. It is thoroughly intelligent up to age-capacity.

How dear such young believers are to our Lord is gauged by his awesome warning against offending them. How terrible a guilt is theirs who turn them away from him! How immensely important he evidently considers the work of bringing young children to trust in him! The reason why I myself lost the simple trust which I had in him as a child was that when I was five years old I stood up in a testimony meeting and with joyful innocence testified that Jesus had taken away my sin-burden, whereupon two maiden ladies sitting just in front of me loudly whispered their sarcastic incredulity: "How ridiculous for a mere child to talk like that!" I could never express the damage it did. Crushed and bewildered, I suddenly doubted the reality of conversion, and began to think it must be a pretense of grown-ups. How silly it now seemed, to think that Jesus loved a little thing like me! Gradually I lost both my faith in him and any desire for him, and grew up to be a godless young worldling.

Let us mark well our Lord's severe warning and learn from it the measureless *preciousness* of little children to him—not only those who have been taught about him and "believe" in him, but all those others who, through no fault of their own, have *not* been taught. Of them all he says, "Whoso shall receive one such little child in my name receiveth me"; and again, "Forbid them not to come to me." Remember again who it is who so speaks. He has the first right to them by creation and redemption, and if he thus treasures them, is not that his guarantee that if they *die* as children they are *saved?*

That brings us to the *third* feature in our Lord's discourse. In Matthew 18:10 he adds that further admonition against *despising* the young. "Take heed that ye despise not one of these little ones; for I say unto you, That in heaven their angels do always behold the face of my Father which is in heaven." A revealing word indeed! Children have guardian angels! Attempts to lessen the meaning of our Lord's words have been, as the scholarly Dean Alford says, "merely to evade the plain sense" of them. What our Lord said is the more notable because it is not loosely plural and general but significantly singular—"*one* of these little ones." There is one of those heavenly guardians for *each* little one.

Nor is that all. Those heavenly watchers are angels with special privilege. "In heaven their angels always behold the face of my Father who is in heaven." According to Oriental custom, only select favorites were allowed to come often into a monarch's presence. But even more, our Lord means that those angels have direct *access* to God, on behalf of earth's little ones, in a way which other angels do not. They are priority servants of the Crown. Such is the importance which God attaches to children. Meanwhile it emerges clearly that at the *death* of each child at least one guardian angel is invisibly present; and as soon as the guileless little one vacates the body, the real child is gently borne away to the best of all nurseries, there to be cherished, nurtured, and tutored in ways infinitely better than any earthly upbringing which could have been provided.

And now, in verses 11 to 14, comes the fourth and final part of our Lord's declaration on infant salvation. It is a crowning parable.

> For the Son of man is come to save that which was lost. How think ye? If a man have an hundred sheep, and one of them be gone astray, doth he not leave the ninety and nine, and goeth into

the mountains, and seeketh that which is gone astray? And if so be that he find it, verily I say unto you, he rejoiceth more of that sheep, than of the ninety and nine which went not astray. Even so it is not the will of your Father which is in heaven, that one of these little ones should perish.

This parable need not be restricted to children, yet the captivating fact is, it was to them that our Lord himself applied it. "It is not the will of your Father that one of these *little ones* should perish." Note that our Lord puts his statement in a negative form. That is, he tells us what the will of God is *not:* "It is not the will of your Father that one of these little ones should *perish.*" The use of the negative in such cases is a rhetorical form of emphasis. For instance, Exodus 20:7 says, "The Lord will *not* hold him guiltless," meaning that the Lord will most surely condemn him as guilty. So, when Jesus here tells us it is *not* the will of God that even one little child should perish, he is accentuating the positive. "It *is* the will of your Father who is in heaven that each of these little ones *should be saved.*"

Let us seize eagerly that assurance. It is God's will that children should be saved: so if they die in infancy they *are* saved. The Good Shepherd came to save *them.* His parable says so. He *died* to save them. They are his by purchase. The Law cannot condemn them, for they have never broken it: and the Cross of Jesus more than answers for all their hereditary disqualifications. The Father's will is now expressed through God the Son—through what he taught and what he wrought. Beyond a doubt, then, those who die as children are *saved.*

What eloquence there often was in the *gestures* by which our Lord complemented his teachings or miracles! He not only healed the leper; he *touched* him. On the evening after his resurrection he not only said to his disciples, "Receive ye the Holy Spirit"; he symbolically *breathed* on them. Now when he spoke his wonderful words about children, in Matthew 18, he also *did* something which put a lovely embroidery on what he said. He "called a little child." Then he "set *him* in the midst" (so it was a little boy). Can you not hear and see it? But there is more. Mark mentions something which Matthew omits. He says that Jesus "set him in the midst . . . and when he had *taken him in his arms* he said to them . . ." Jesus preached that sermon with the wee laddie actually in his arms! Those arms were the arms of God. Let those arms speak as well as those lips. They tell us that when our little ones pass from this earthly scene we may sing with consoling certainty the words of the old hymn,

> *Safe in the arms of Jesus,*
> *Safe on his gentle breast,*
> *There, by his love o'ershaded,*
> *Sweetly my soul shall rest.*

THE THEOLOGICAL WHY AND WHEREFORE

In view of our Lord's decisive word on infant salvation some of us may judge that no further argument is needed. It certainly is enough for me. Yet for our clearer understanding perhaps we ought to grasp the "why and wherefore" behind it; that is, the evangelical *theology* of it as revealed in the New Testament *epistles.*

There were many truths which our Lord could not teach even the apostles during his ministry on earth; truths that could not have been understood before his crucifixion and resurrection. To the inner circle of his disciples he said, "I have yet many things to say unto you, but ye cannot bear them now" (John 16:12). However, he immediately added, "Howbeit when he, the Spirit of truth, is come, he will guide you into all the truth." That, indeed, is what the Holy Spirit soon afterwards *did* through inspired penmen. Practically all the great truths later developed in the epistles are found in *germ* in our Lord's own teachings. Moreover, those germinal teachings are developed in the epistles in the light of our Lord's atoning death and resurrection. That is, they assume completion as evangelical doctrine.

That is true of the teaching about infant salvation. As we have now seen, our Lord himself tells us the *fact* of their salvation; but in the epistles we learn the great truth underlying that fact, namely, *they are saved by the atonement of Christ.* Already we have touched on that supposedly problematical aspect of child-salvation: the fact that although infants are not sinners by self-committed acts, they inherit a perverted *nature.* They do not need "justification" (the *legal* side of salvation), for of course they have no guilt; but they *do* need "regeneration" (the *spiritual* aspect) because of hereditary sin-proclivity. Furthermore, although they have no guilt, they are part of the Adamic race, and therefore (so it is supposed) fall under the *racial* condemnation. How does the justice of God relate itself to *that?*

If we would see how the provisions of the Gospel cover that problem, we need to know the first eight chapters of Paul's epistle to the Romans. Those chapters clarify what we may call the divine "reason" or philosophy of salvation. Here I advert to one paragraph only: Romans 5:12-21. This paragraph confirms our earlier remark that our racial fall in Adam did *not* make us "transgressors." There is no such thing as hereditary transgression. We do not become transgressors until we reach responsible adulthood and knowingly commit wrong. That, and *only* that, makes us transgressors and consequently guilty.

But although we do not inherit transgression, we *do* inherit those other results of Adam's disobedience—mortality, spiritual death, and moral sin-bias. The complex tragedy is that the righteous penalty on Adam could not be inflicted without involving his posterity—not unless God could have obliterated the law of heredity, in which case the organic unity of the race would have been destroyed, and the redemptive purpose of God aborted. That which fell on Adam as a judgment was passed on to his posterity as an inherited bondage. Paul calls it the "bondage of corruption" (Rom. 8:21). Human babes are no more responsible for that fatal legacy of corruption than you and I are. God knows that, far better than any of us; and his answer to it is the *Savior,* our Lord Jesus Christ, one of whose titles is "the Second Adam."

There are now two Adams, the old and the new. Just as we were all involved in the fall of the *first* Adam, so, by divine grace, do we all come under the provision of salvation through the *second* Adam, Jesus. His atonement covers us all in the sense that it covers *all* that we have involuntarily inherited from the *first* Adam. Yes, Jesus, God incarnate, the new representative Man, vicariously bore the penalty and guilt of the whole race in his substitutionary self-sacrifice. Only the infinite God himself could make such a full, final-and-forever atonement; but he *did* it. Thus the sin-barrier between God and man is removed. All who hear that Good News and receive the dear Savior are thereby saved for ever.

All this has an illuminative bearing on the salvation of those who die as infants. They were sold to sin and death by the first Adam, without their knowing it or willing it. They were also redeemed by the "precious blood" of the *second* Adam, without their knowing it or asking it. Because of that, not only do they have angel attendants, but as they pass from here to yonder the Spirit of God renews their moral and spiritual nature so that from their infancy they become "new creatures" in Christ. Scriptural instances of such renewal by the Holy Spirit in the young, even in babes, are not lacking. When the angel Gabriel preannounced the birth of John, our Lord's forerunner, he said, "He shall be filled with the Holy Ghost, even from his mother's womb" (Luke 1:15). A similar instance is that of Jeremiah, to whom God said, "Before thou camest forth out of the womb I sanctified thee" (Jer. 1:5). We think of young Samuel and others, all serving to illume the precious truth that those who die as infants are redeemed by the precious blood of Jesus, regenerated by the Holy Spirit and "made meet to be partakers of the inheritance of the saints in light" (Col. 1:12).

The Scriptures do not hint at any such plan of salvation for the fallen angels. Among them there is no heredity or organic unity of genus. There is no procreation. There are no parent angels or children angels. There is no inheritance of nature or disposition or qualities. The angels are not "born." They do not "grow." Each angel is a direct creation of God. Each angel who sinned did so *of* himself and *for* himself and *to* himself, without involving any other of his kind. But with the human race all were involved in one and in each other. Therefore there was the divine provision of "the Lamb slain from the foundation of the world" (Rev. 13:8). The "new covenant" sealed with the blood of Calvary makes all human infants the inalienable beneficiaries of its provisions. It guarantees their eternal salvation. What we say is well grounded in that fifth chapter of Romans. Read it until you really grip it and it grips *you;* and you will never again doubt that all who die in infancy are *saved.*

WHAT OF THEIR PRESENT STATE?

There is a further question: *May we know the present state of the little ones who die?* There is much that we are evidently not meant to know about them at present. Yet there is that which may be reliably deduced from the biblical data.

First, let us realize that although they are no longer here, they *grow.* They grow normally and uninterruptedly to human maturity. We must not harbor the strange fancy that because they die as children they *stay* as children in the realm beyond. In Matthew 21:16, our Lord quotes from Psalm 8, "Out of the mouths of babes and sucklings thou [God] hast perfected praise." C. H. Spurgeon asks, "Does not that text seem to say that in heaven there shall be 'perfect praise' rendered to God by a multitude of cherubs who were here on earth—your little ones fondled in your bosom—and then suddenly snatched away to heaven?" Unless I misunderstand the beloved preacher, he voices the idea that those who die as children *remain* children in that fair clime yonder.

Let us do away with that misconception forever. If our dear bairns had lingered with us here, we would have watched them develop from cradle to manhood and womanhood, mind and body progressing in union with each other. When they left us they certainly did not take their little bodies to heaven with them, but their minds, their real selves, develop, unfold, learn, and grow just as they would have done if they had remained on earth. We are not just roving in romantic sentiment when we say that in heaven there are nurseries and kindergartens far better than any down here.

Sorrowing fathers and mothers, ponder that. Those precious little treasures whose eyes death gently closed on earth wakened amid that heavenly homeland where, without any interruption, their mental development has proceeded, and where, in an environment exempt from all taint, disease, tears, and shadows, they are tutored for exquisite ministries in the palace of the King of kings.

As a corollary of that, be persuaded of this (gratefully so): those who have gone there as infants will not meet us *as such* when we ourselves pass into the Beyond. The following quotation from an author whom we will leave anonymous is quite out of kilter. "Ere long you will be received at heaven's gate by *those very little ones* who have gone before." Welcome us they surely will, but not in the stuntedness of fixed immaturity. Listen, disconsolate parent: that bonny wee son who was taken from you will always be your son; that cherub-faced little girl who slipped away from your embrace will always be your daughter: yet in your deepest heart and truest reason would you wish him or her to remain in perpetual childhood? No! Wait until you see God's finished product. Wait until that "bright and cloudless morning" of which J. M. Black's hymn speaks, when you will see and recognize your precious one, still yours by distinguishing similarities, but having developed into supernally superb adulthood, and fulfilling exalted heavenly ministries beyond your most golden dreams! When at last, in the transfiguring explanations and answers of that promised daybreak, you see how wise and gracious has been God's purpose behind permitted bereavement on earth, you will break into singing with millions of others the doxology, "Praise God from whom all blessings flow."

When the advent trumpet reverberates around the arching skies, and Christ descends in flaming splendor, and the Christian dead are raised, and the living saints are translated, all the redeemed in Christ will be "clothed upon" with their immortal resurrection bodies. That will appropriately include all those who have died as children. As we have said elsewhere, there is no physiological problem involved in the resurrection body. It will be similar in *structure* to the flesh-and-blood body occupied by the Christian believer in this present life, but it will *not* be identical in *texture*. All disfigurements will have been erased, and perfect beauty will glorify it without obscuring its personal identity, while all those distinguishing traits which have been loved on earth will be emphasized and sublimated. As 1 John 3:2 says, "We shall be like him" (Jesus). Or as 1 Corinthians 15:49 puts it, "We shall bear the image of the heavenly." In the case of those who died as children it will not be the immaturely dead child-body which is restored, but that body in its normal structural development, celestialized like the bodies of all the other raptured saints.

IS IT WELL WITH THE CHILD?

Long ago, the prophet Elisha asked the bereaved Shunammite woman, "Is it well with the child?" She replied (with her infant son lying suddenly dead at home), "It is well."

91

Bereaved parents, take comfort. If the Bible is the Word of God (as indeed it is), then however painful the present severance from your departed little one may be, remember that in the most wonderful way it is "well with the child." Lean your heart upon the Good Shepherd who, as the Scripture says, "Gathers the lambs with his arm." On that morning of mornings yet to be, every question will be answered and every dark perplexity dispersed. Indeed, we shall not need to wait until then if we are by faith united to the Lord Jesus; for if we "pass over" before his return to earth, death will be our translation to the "Father's house" of "many mansions," where we shall no longer see "through a glass darkly" but "face to face."

Meanwhile, if little ones are taken from us, like unopened flowerets plucked from the garden by an invisible hand, let us try to discern a *gracious purpose* even through our tears. Each dear little one taken from us is meant to be a tender link with heaven, to help wean our hearts from too much love of earthly things. "Where your treasure is," says Jesus, "there will your heart be also."

Not long ago, some dear friends of mine lost their tiny firstborn, and in writing them at that time I found my thoughts shaping themselves into the following verses which may serve as a fitting close to our reflections on this tender subject.

> *Lord Jesus, you were born on earth*
> *As lowly Mary's little Son;*
> *You have a kinship by your birth*
> *With every other little one.*
>
> *In loving welcome you have said,*
> *"Let little children come to me";*
> *And when they die they are not dead,*
> *They wake in heav'n with you to be.*
>
> *Nor do they static there remain,*
> *They grow in mind as if still here;*
> *And fairer stature there attain*
> *Amid that sinless higher sphere.*

We yet shall see them, lovely grown,
  Fulfilling heavenly ministries;
And in that day our hearts will own
  The love behind earth's mysteries.

And all such children called away
  Are tender links from here to there,
Until that glad reunion day
  When we with them your heaven share.

J. S. B.

FIVE

WHY IS DEATH GAIN TO THE CHRISTIAN?

Eye hath not seen, nor ear heard, neither have entered into the heart of man, the things which God hath prepared for them that love him.

1 Corinthians 2:9

An inheritance incorruptible, and undefiled, and that fadeth not away, reserved in heaven for you.

1 Peter 1:4

Not just one glimpse, but forever,
Forever "at home" with Thee,
To live in that beautiful homeland,
Its splendors unfading to see!
Yet in all that wonderful heaven
Will anything ever efface
That longed-for enrapturing moment,
My first, first sight of his face?

Anonymous

If this chapter sounds dangerously like a "sermon," maybe that is just what it is: so get ready! I have my eye on a gripping little sentence in Paul's epistle to the Philippians. He says, "For to me to live is Christ, and *to die is gain*" (1:21). If that does not halt us in our tracks and set us questioning, nothing ever will.

Think of it: "To die is gain"! Was Paul's eager imagination running away with him? Did he really mean it? Did he have solid grounds for saying, "To die is gain"? That is the exact opposite of what our modern Western world would say. To the man of the world, it is of all losses the most irretrievable, for at one stroke he loses all his possessions, his pursuits, his friends and loved ones—everything. Even if he believes in soul-survival beyond bodily death, he passes to it in stark ignorance, in disembodied nudity, and in nameless dread.

When the millionaire Vanderbilt died, the usual question was asked, "How much has he left?" Somebody gave an unusual reply: "He's left *all*." Yes, to the merely natural man, death is the finally pauperizing loss. He leaves *all*. No matter how many flowers may be heaped on the coffin, and however lavish may be the encomiums uttered over

97

the corpse, the dirge which clings around his funeral is, "To die is *loss.*"

All who live in disregard of God and of his written Word should be persistently reminded of this. Nothing bankrupts men so completely and inexorably as death. With one icy breath it withers the strength of the warrior and defaces the charm of the enchantress. With one press of its iron fingers, death wrenches the merchant from his hoarded profits, strips the glitter from earthly royalty, rips away the trappings of aristocracy, and chokes the loud brag of the inflated dictator forever.

France never produced a more brilliant opponent of Christianity than the versatile Voltaire. Toward the end of his mortal span, with a colorful career behind him but disgusted with the cruel ironies of earthly life, and now alarmed at the prospect of death, he wrote: "I wish I had never been born." His sense of desolation was deep and chilling. Toward the end he was so afraid of death that he said to his doctor, "I will give you half of what I am worth if you will give me six more months of life." Voltaire's melancholy plight has been that of many another such as he. To all such worldlings death is the super-loss, utter and irremediable. The flickering taper is quenched forever. The candle is snuffed out in smoky darkness. The battery is exhausted; and in that instant every thrill and ambition is extinguished with it.

What a contrast is Paul's exultation, "To die is *gain*"! Who but a Christian like Paul could say it and intelligently mean it, based on certified guarantees? We know, of course, that during the Second World War there were Japanese suicide squads who rushed to death in the fanatical belief that dying for the emperor would immediately sweep them to some fantastic Shangri-la in the Beyond. But those of us who know anything about Shintoism know that such an idea was merely a vaporous delusion with nothing behind it but the fictitious divinity of the now-disappeared emperor. We also know that the Koran promises Muhammadan men (not women) a voluptuous paradise on the other side of death with "gardens of pleasure . . . goblets of wine . . . couches of ease . . . and large-eyed maidens" to gratify sensuous desire; all of which is obviously nothing but carnal invention. At the time this book is being penned there are mentally intoxicated suicide zealots in the Middle East who for the sake of killing Jews and Americans blast themselves into eternity in the mad belief that their action will usher them to a dazzling reward. How inanely gullible can men be!

Far removed from all such fatuous delusion is Paul's glowing but thoughtful affirmation, "To die is gain," for it has behind it the demonstrated sanity and authentic facts of the Christian revelation, especially the invulnerable fact of our Lord's bodily resurrection. Paul knew, as we now do, how soundly factual are the bases of our Christian faith and hope. He had actually encountered the risen Savior on the Damascus road. He had been the vehicle through which that living Master had worked thousands of healing miracles, even the raising of the dead. He had deeply experienced the infilling Holy Spirit in his life and through his ministry. He had searched the sacred Scriptures with scholarly carefulness and had found in them the birth, life, miracles, death, resurrection, and ascension of Christ all clearly foretold *centuries in advance* through the Hebrew prophets. He knew how true were the fulfillments of those prophecies, and how divinely attested were the basic truths of the Christian gospel. And to crown it all, at one point God had given Paul a kind of glimpse into heaven similar to the apostle John's visions on the Isle of Patmos. Yes, Paul had glimpsed something of the rapture into which our Lord's faithful servants pass when they vacate the mortal body. All that was behind Paul's victory cry, "To die is *gain.*"

The glad word rings down to us through the *Anno Domini* centuries: "To die is gain"; and with good reason it sets many of us asking, "*Why* is death gain to the Christian?" The very question spurs eager thought; and answers come readily to mind. There are four big reasons why death is gain to those of us who know and love the Savior. It is so because of: (1) the One to whom it takes us; (2) the place to which it bears us; (3) the state to which it lifts us; (4) the rewards to which it leads us.

THE FIRST REASON

In the first place, death is gain to us Christians because of *the One to whom it takes us*. Scarcely has Paul said, "To die is gain" before he adds, "I am in a strait betwixt two, having a desire to depart, and to be with *Christ;* which is far better. . . ." The one and only thought which could set Paul wistfully wishing to leave his wonderful ministry on earth was that of being with *Christ* in heaven.

That prospect of being with our Lord Jesus yonder will mean more to some Christians than to others. Our desire to be with him *there* will correspond with the degree to which we love and prize him *here*. To those who love him even now as their all-in-all, the meeting with him over there will be sheer rapture. To others, perhaps, it will not be quite that intensity of bliss—at least not in the first moment of meeting. Nevertheless this is true, that in each born-again believer there is such love for the Lord Jesus that the anticipation of seeing him face to face is deeply stirring. Most certainly the contemplation of being with that adorable Savior is the *first* thing that makes heaven magnetic.

How could it be otherwise? Did he not love us before ever we loved him? Did he not show wondrous compassion for us when we were loathsomely ugly in the moral leprosy of sin? Did he not for our sake make the vast descent from heaven's sapphire throne to Calvary's gory cross? Has he not bought us back from the slave market, and flung his arms of rescue around us, and restored us to the heavenly Father, making us free again as the reinstated "sons of

God?" Has he not cleansed and healed and transformed us? Is he not the kindest, purest, noblest, sublimest character we have ever known?—the *ne plus ultra* of moral beauty, the fairest of the fair, the "altogether lovely?" Does he not indwell us, comforting, caring, strengthening, companioning us with never-failing constancy? How can we help but love him gratefully for all he did to redeem us? How can we help but love him adoringly for all that he is in himself? How can we help but love him for all that he has now become to us through years of experience? A thousand times, yes, it is the prospect of being "with Christ" which makes heaven alluring and death "gain." We sing with Bernard of Clairvaux,

> *Jesus, the very thought of thee*
> *With sweetness fills my breast;*
> *But sweeter far thy face to see,*
> *And in thy presence rest.*

Christian, try to imagine what it must be, to be with *him*. Because he is infinite in all his attributes, not only is his love boundless, it is so individualizing that he loves *each* of us in careful distinguishment. If that seems hard to grasp, it is only so because our finite minds cannot grasp the infinite. He prizes every outreach of our hearts toward him. Picture it, if you can: we shall be with *him,* the Crown Prince of the universe, yet the dearest, kindest, humblest, tenderest, purest, and most self-sacrificing Friend our hearts could ever know! Could there possibly be any truer heaven than the sunrise of his smile, the sympathetic light of his eyes, the joy-communicating touch of his hand, the rich music of his voice, his confidential communing with us, his sharing of his thoughts with us, his heart-to-heart interpreting to us the basic mystery of our being—why we were created, his own secret name for us, and his special ministry for us through the unfolding ages? And what will it mean, that all the while he walks and talks with us he is leading us to "fountains of living waters"? Will it not be a "heaven of heavens" to be with *him?*

> *The King there in his beauty*
>   *In shadeless light is seen;*
> *It were a well-spent journey*
>   *Tho' seven deaths lay between:*
> *To praise him mid the myriads*
>   *Who on Mount Zion stand,*
> *Will be my heaven of heavens*
>   *In Immanuel's land.*

THE SECOND REASON

In conjunction with all that, death is "gain" to the Christian because of *the place to which it bears us.* It wings us to a place called "heaven." There are those who seem to think that heaven is no more than a subjective condition of bliss which will be wrought within us; but they have not sufficiently appraised the biblical evidence. Colossians 3:1 says, "Seek those things which are above, where Christ sitteth on the right hand of God." Such wording indicates a locale where the divine presence and government are centered. As such, "heaven" (singular) is to be distinguished from the "heavens" (plural). As mentioned earlier, that difference between "heaven" and "heavens" is clearly shown in Hebrews 4:14 and 9:24. In the former, our Lord "passed *through* the heavens" (see ASV, et al.) whereas in the latter he "entered . . . *into heaven itself*" (singular), to appear in the *presence of God* for us. So "heaven itself" is somehow, in a concentrated way, the "presence of God." It was there that the risen Lord returned after his resurrection, for Mark 16:19 says, "He was received up into *heaven,* and sat on the right hand of God." It is there that he now is, for 1 Peter 3:22 says, "Who is gone into *heaven,* and is on the right hand of God; angels and authorities and powers being made subject unto him." It is from there that he will come back to earth in the splendor of his second advent, for 2 Thessalonians 1:7 says, "The Lord Jesus shall be revealed from *heaven* with his mighty angels."

Yes, "heaven" (singular) is a *place*. It is the place to which death transports all true Christian believers—and what a place! The first epistle of Peter describes it as "an inheritance incorruptible, and undefiled, and that fadeth not away" (1:4)—that is, bloom without blight, felicity without flaw, delight without decay. Colossians 1:12 calls it "the inheritance of the saints in *light*"—that is, in the light of God's immediate presence, where there is not the faintest flicker of unholy thought or desire or fear or doubt or anxiety, but all is shadowless serenity. As already mentioned, Revelation, chapter 7, gives us a glimpse of it in Patmos pen-photography. There they are, the translated saints in heaven, "before the throne and before the Lamb," clothed with white robes and waving victory-palms; hungering and thirsting no more; with every tear wiped away, and drinking "living waters" of immortality.

What a picture! We must not over-literalize it, but what it represents is unmistakable: open vision of the divine glory, unsullied holiness, finalized victory, heavenly ministries, highest fulfillment of all pure hopes, ageless vitality, every sorrow healed, sinless rapture. Gone forever the burden of mortal flesh and earthly troubles, weakness, pain, temptation, grief, anxiety, limitation, frustration. What a transition—from here to there; from this to that; from now to then! Amid a period of excessive strain and weakness Paul had been granted a vision of it (2 Cor. 12:2-4). He had learned "sacred secrets" (as Moffatt translates it). He was never quite the same afterward. The wonder of it was still before his inward eyes when he later wrote, "I have a desire to depart and to be with Christ." How could he say otherwise than "to die is *gain*"? And how can we Christians today, amid the alternating songs and sighs of this present pilgrimage, help longing for that beatific answer to the deepest yearnings of our humanhood?

Artistic Spring awakes the flowers,
And paints the landscape fair,
But Autumn wilts the gayest bowers,
And Winter strips them bare:
Oh, for that land of light and love
Free from all blight and gloom!
Oh, for that paradise above
Where flowers unfading bloom!

The questing eye and supple limb
Of youth's romantic hour.
How swiftly gone! Its vigors dim
In quickly jaded power:
Oh, for the life of ageless day,
Mounting on eagle's wings!
Oh, for the youth beyond decay,
To serve my King of Kings!

THE THIRD REASON

In the third place, death is "gain" to the Christian because of *the state to which it lifts us.* Not only shall we be in a superbly different realm; we ourselves will be correspondingly changed. Our present form of mind and heart will undergo metamorphosis into a superior quality of knowing and feeling which is beyond present imagining. Not only shall we be in heaven, but heaven will be in *us.* Our perfected happiness will spring from perfected holiness. Our moral and spiritual nature will be in faultless harmony with that exquisite environment. In our inmost being we ourselves will have become heavenly.

Have you ever tried to imagine what it will be like to have a mind that is radiant light with no darkness at all?—with never a selfish thought, never a wish that is not translucently pure, never a motive toward others that is not transparently sincere, never a fleck of envy or jealousy or resentment or unholy desire or competitiveness; never a tremor of doubt, never a wisp of fear, or flutter of pride, or whiff of self-assertiveness, but the whole interior life filled with love in the sense of selfless "otherism"? When we are all in that state of inwrought sinlessness there cannot be misunderstandings, dissensions, or rivalries of any kind except rivalry in blessing each other. In that condition I can never find myself plaintively wondering if my Lord Jesus loves someone else more than he loves myself. No, because one of the very elements of my joy will be my so sharing his love for others that the more he expresses his love to them, the richer my own joy will be; and the more will others rejoice in his love to *me*. But I must desist, for I am trying to describe what at present is indescribable. When at last we are there, perhaps the glory of it will make it difficult for us to think that we ever were what we now are!

That enrapturing metamorphosis, however, will not be effected in us by death itself. It is strange how the idea clings that the change will be wrought in us simply by our being without the mortal body. For instance, one distinguished expositor says, "There will come a time when I stand before God in all the holiness of Jesus Christ . . . with the root of sin in me destroyed forever, since it passes away from me with the death of this body." That idea must be rejected. It makes the body itself the seat of sin, and we are back among the Gnostics. The body is non-sentient matter, and is not in itself sinful.

Sin is a perversion of our *moral* nature. It inheres in the *mind*. No discarding of the merely physical can destroy an innate mental propensity. Any moral, mental, spiritual change wrought in you or me, whether in this present life or in the life beyond, is the work of the Holy Spirit. Who on this side of the grave can say just what the Spirit does in the disembodied Christian immediately after the body is vacated? We know the reality of his work of regeneration here on earth. We know how (sometimes with whelming suddenness) he can effect a deep-going renewal of one's whole inner life when there is full yieldedness to Christ. Many outstanding Christians have left testimony to that. Yet all such experiences must be eclipsed by his culminating intervention at the moment of our discarding the body.

Concurrently with that, how mentally revolutionizing such a passing from the body must be! What must it be, suddenly to find ourselves existing without a body—the body which has hitherto clothed each of us from the moment we came into existence?

In that coming translation we shall suddenly begin to see without eyes, hear without ears, and be aware of presences by purely spiritual susceptibilities. Instead of seeing, hearing, feeling, touching, sensing, all by separate organs, there will be an all-in-one cognizance of realities. God will no longer be known indirectly and indistinctly through processes of reason, or as he is now explained to our present limited grasp in the written Scriptures; but in an instant there will be a direct apprehending of God and of spiritual meanings. As Paul says, "Then shall I *know* even as also I am known," i.e., directly. "Now we see through a glass, darkly; but then face to face." What it is to "see" without the body none can at present explain, but it is then that the words of Isaiah 33:17 will have cloudless fulfillment: "Thine eyes shall *see* the king in his beauty."

What consolation, to know that in the very instant of my disembodiment I shall experience a complete envelopment by the Holy Spirit, the heavenly "Comforter"! In that transition (I incline to think) there will come, all-in-one, such a realization of sinfulness, and such a consciousness of utter salvation from it, and such a compelling vision of our Savior, as we never knew on earth. It will effect in us such an utter yieldedness to him, accompanied by such a renewal of our whole being, that the release and rapture will be instantaneously all-suffusing. As with an electric flash we shall then know to utmost capacity that for the Christian "to die is gain." As the old Sankey hymn says,

Then we shall be what we should be,
And we will be what we would be,
Things that are not now nor could be,
Then shall be our own.

THE FOURTH REASON

Finally, death is "gain" to the Christian because of *the re-wards to which it leads us.* Heaven will hold gracious reward for whatever service we have rendered to our royal Master. Not that we serve him for *any* reward. How could we? The very thought of *his* giving reward to *us* is embarrassing. At best we are "unprofitable servants." Yet that will make his rewards the more treasured. No sincere service will be overlooked. In one place Jesus says that even "a cup of cold water" given in his name "shall not lose its reward." In another place he assures those who endure persecution for his sake, "Great is your reward in heaven." Every sacrifice for him will have superlative recompense there.

For one thing, in heaven we are going to wear *crowns.* In James 1:12 faithful ones are promised a "crown of *life.*" In 1 Peter 5:4, they are promised a "crown of glory." In 2 Timothy 4:8, the promise is a "crown of righteouness." In 1 Corinthians 9:25 it is an "incorruptible crown." Frankly, I do not care to picture myself wearing a crown. I am not made that way. It could seem almost comically incongruous to me. How could I ever presume to wear a crown in *his* presence who once wore a crown of thorns for me? I say to myself that if ever Jesus should put a crown on *my* head, all I could do would be to take it off quickly but reverently and lay it with tears of gratitude at his nail-pierced feet.

Yet perhaps I am wrong, because those promised "crowns" are not to be interpreted literally. They are not material crowns which give me regal power over less privileged beings. No, they are symbolic. The "crown of *life*" means reigning in final victory over death. The "crown of *righteousness*" means reigning in final victory over sin. The "crown of *glory*" means reigning in final victory over all decay. Yes, those crowns mean immortal life, utter holiness, unwithering bloom. *Those* crowns are worn by the pure in heart, by the meek and humble. They were never made to fit swelled heads! All of us may well covet to wear *those* crowns; for all the time we are wearing them they will be gleaming testimonials to "him that loved us, and washed us from our sins in his own blood, and hath made us kings and priests unto God" (Rev. 1:5-6).

Moreover, along with those crowns there are other rewards which make death "gain" to born-again believers. There will be the rewarding joy of rendering heavenly *service* to our dear King. Revelation 7:15 says of the saints yonder that they "serve him day and night in his temple." *That* temple is coextensive with heaven. Vast and varied, what spacious scope it provides for all kinds of consecrated activities! We are meant to understand that there will be no monotonous immobility yonder. To a healthy mind, activity in service and accomplishment is enjoyment. Few of us would feel drawn to heaven if it were a perpetual lazing alongside purling streams, fanned by balmy zephyrs in dreamy air, or idling eternity away in nothing but psalm-singing.

Heaven is a world of tireless energy, ministry, opportunity, inventive occupation, and self-fulfillment. David will humor even more melodious strains from his harp. Isaiah will soar to still higher heights of poetry. Isaac Newton will have a whole universe to investigate. The artificer will make nobler furnishings with better tools for the sanctuary and dwellings of that super-sensory realm. Warriors will be given far higher conquests than storming strongholds. Doctors will be given far higher careers than battling bodily disease and signing death certificates. There will be no enemies to fight, no ailments to heal, no corpses to shroud. All will have ministries corresponding with their higher state of mind and elevated capacities.

Along with all that, there will be the reward of *fellowship* surpassing anything we have known on earth. All around us will be that shining "cloud of witnesses"—the redeemed of all the centuries, all serving the same Savior-King, and all with pure hearts welcoming our participation of heaven with them, just as our own hearts will leap with pleasure at such congenial communion. Moses will be there, grander and meeker than ever. David will be there, eager to learn all about our experience with the "Good Shepherd" and to sing Psalm 23 for us accompanied with music from better strings than he ever strummed in old Judea. John will be there, to tell us all kinds of details about his Patmos apocalypses which he could not put into his Book of the Revelation. Paul, the apostle excelsior, will be there without any lingering ophthalmic trouble, and no longer seeing "through a glass, darkly." Perhaps while Paul converses with us, angels will group around, for as 1 Peter 1:12 says, "the angels desire to look into" these things; and perhaps Peter himself will interject, "Did I not tell you that it would be 'joy unspeakable and full of glory'?" (1 Pet. 1:8).

Indeed, there will be such an "innumerable company of angels" there, and such a countless "assembly" of "the church of the firstborn" whose names are "written in heaven" (Heb. 12:22-23) that eternity will seem too short for fellowship with them all! It will all be fellowship without the slightest alloy of misunderstanding or variance. There will be no Reverend So-and-So to preach on such themes as "Why I Am a Calvinist," or "Why We Should All Be Baptists," or "The Case for Episcopalianism," or "Where the Post-Tribulationists Went Wrong." All will be in perfect agreement, and all will be immersed in love for the same dear Savior-Master. Nor will there be any jealousy there. Nay, not one breath of it could live in that pure environ. There will be no question as to why some vessels seem large and some less; for each will be filled to capacity with love and joy.

Added to all that, there will be the reward of *reunion*

with our own departed loved ones who were near and dear to us in this present world. They will be just the same in their personal identity as when they were here with us, except that every wrinkle, every blemish, every disfigurement, every mark of age or weakness will have gone forever; while all those character traits which were so dear to us will have been emphasized into lovelier expression. In the transition through death from here to yonder there will be neither abruption nor diminution of consciousness. As we have earlier said, there will be neither any fading of identity nor any blurring of personality. You will always be you. I shall always be I. So will it be with all those dear ones who on earth have lived and loved in the Lord. Instead of obliterating identity or personality, the translation from here to there *sublimates* them, perpetuating and perfecting every feature of beauty.

Oh, there will be such reunions there! For so many of us, particularly those of us who are now older and have more links with that invisible haven, the coming reunion is one of the tenderer aspects which make death "gain" to the Christian. Sometimes the waiting days on earth seem too long. With gratitude for a lifetime of divine favors to us, and with longings for that final consummation, we find ourselves singing with the late John Henry Newman,

> So long thy care has blest me, sure it still
>   Will lead me on,
> O'er moor and fen, o'er crag and torrent, till
>   The night is gone;
> And with the morn those dear, dear faces smile
> Which I have loved on earth, and lost awhile.

"What more shall we say?" Time would fail us to tell of all the other inducements which beckon us yonder. We blend our hearts and voices with Paul's, and sing again with him, *"to die is gain."*

SIX

THE "SOUL-SLEEP" THEORY

I regret that the controversial must intrude into these studies, but I can hardly avoid it if I am to deal faithfully and squarely with such a subject as "the other side of death." Even among those who, like myself, believe the Bible to be the inspired Word of God, there are differences of interpretation resulting in different *theories*. Let it be understood therefore that even where we strongly differ and are most outspoken, we speak with esteem toward the persons who hold and teach theories of which we keenly disapprove.

J. S. B.

Some see too little, some too much,
  In what the Scriptures say,
And some with scholar's subtle touch
  "Explain" the sense away:
The plainest texts of Holy Writ
  Are trimmed by artful pen,
And tinkered with until they fit
  False theories of men:
Thus strangest novelties are found
  Within God's Holy Book,
And specious errors now abound
  Wherever we may look.

J. S. B.

I wonder how many of us are acquainted with the soul-sleep theory: the teaching that between death and yet-future resurrection the soul (the real person) is "asleep." That supposed sleep, however, is not ordinary nighttime slumber but an utter blackout of consciousness. There are two main forms of the soul-sleep theory: (1) the Seventh-Day Adventist, and (2) the Bullingerite. We shall examine them in this order.

SEVENTH-DAY ADVENTIST VERSION

Let me pay tribute to the sincerity of the Seventh-Day Adventists. A sincerer body we could hardly find. Moreover, they are masters at putting their case over. They are not to be classed with heretical sects like the so-called Jehovah's Witnesses, the Christian Scientists, and others which deny the deity of our Lord Jesus, the personalness of the Holy Spirit, and the triunity of God. The Seventh-Day Adventists are soundly trinitarian and wish to be known as evangelical.

Albeit, that does not make the doctrines peculiar to them

right. Some of the worst heretics in church history have been the sincerest. That did not excuse their error; it made them the more dangerous. Long ago, Nicodemus asked his fellow Pharisees, "Doth our law judge any man before it hear him?" So, let us hear some representative spokesmen of Seventh-Day Adventism.

In 1952, at an outstanding two-week conference in Tacoma Park, Maryland, the Adventist theology was reviewed and reenunciated by chosen speakers of high repute. All the weighty utterances were published in two large volumes entitled *Our Firm Foundation.* The speakers were masters of polemics and lucid statement; so in those two composite volumes we have the official voice of Seventh-Day Adventism. One of the ablest contributions is that by W. L. Emmerson entitled "Life Only through Christ," its subject being life, death, soul-sleep, and final destiny. It well sets forth the case for their soul-sleep theory.

His first concern is to refute those who believe in the immortality of the soul; so he tells us that the "breath" which God breathed, by which man became a "living soul," was no different from the "breath" by which all the lower animals became living souls. To support this he quotes Genesis 1:20-21, 24, 30, and 7:21-22, also Ecclesiastes 3:19. Those texts lead him to say: "We can thus come to no other conclusion from the biblical account of man's creation and later comments on his nature than that there is not the slightest evidence of his possession of any non-material 'something' that assures to him a survival of physical death not credited to the rest of the animal kingdom." So man, according to Mr. Emmerson, although superior in *degree* from the lower animals, is essentially the same as they in *nature* and in the kind of *death* they die.

But surely such reasoning has blinkers on its eyes. It fails to see all kinds of evidence to the contrary both righthand and left. Let me draw a ten-point difference between man and all the lower animals. I believe it will demonstrate with certitude that man is *essentially* different.

114

1. Man was created individually and solitarily. The lower animals were not; they were created collectively and simultaneously in their various categories. They did not originate in one single primigenial. The lions did not all come from one original carnivore. The oxen did not all come from one original bovine quadruped. The whales and porpoises and dolphins did not all come from one aquatic cetacean. The eagles and falcons and nightingales did not all come from one original avian progenitor, and so on. No; all of those more or less sentient creatures had their beginning together in one multiple act of God. No individual "breathing" of God was necessary for the kind of existence which they were to have. As Delitzsch says, "The origin of their soul was coincident with that of their corporeality, and their life was merely the individualization of the universal life with which all matter was filled at the beginning by the Spirit of God." *Why* was man created in such solitary difference if his essential life was identical with that of the beasts?

2. Man was the product of a special deliberation within the Triunity of the Godhead. See Genesis 1:26: "And God said, Let us make man . . ." There is nothing like it elsewhere in the Genesis account of beginnings. Why, then, this halt and divine conference unless man was to be special, unique, and deeply *different* from all other earthly creatures?

3. Man was created in the "image" and "likeness" of God (Gen. 1:26). That is nowhere said of the creatures lower than man. Any such suggestion would be fantastic. There is not the faintest wisp of it in the Bible. That was why God gave man "dominion" over all the other creatures—because although man was one with them in his physical life, he was *not* one with them in his *spiritual* nature. See Genesis 1:27 again: "So God created man *in his own image*. . . ." How unmistakably *that* distinguishes man from all the other creatures!

In what way, then, is man in "the image of God"? Not (as many think) because man is a trinity of body, soul, and

115

spirit, for God does not have a material body, much less a flesh and blood body. Man's "likeness" to his Creator is in his mental, moral, and spiritual nature; which means that instead of being essentially *like* the lower animals, he is essentially *different* from them.

4. Man alone has *intellect,* a reasoning power far above all mere animal instinct and intuition. Even when the evolution hypothesis was shouting its loudest, one of its most able proponents, Professor Huxley, conceded that between the lowest man and the highest beast there is "an enormous gulf, a divergence practically infinite." *That* is no mere difference in "degree." Think further: the mind of an animal cannot reason beyond instinct, beyond the earthly, sensory, momentary. The human intellect can reason, know, and grasp realities beyond earth, time, and sense; and can contemplate the spiritual, eternal, divine. That is a difference in *nature.* Those attributes of human intellect are not something which man has merely *more* of than the lower animals. All the creatures other than man are absolutely without them. Yet our Seventh-Day Adventist apologist tells us, "There is no added 'something' in man that is not possessed by other creatures."

5. Again, man has *moral consciousness,* and along with it that distinguishing inner arbiter, "conscience." Man has an innate sense of right and wrong; of "ought" and "ought not." It is an inherent ingredient of man's nature. It is a faculty which is either there or not there. In man it is *there.* In the lower creatures it is *not.* That distinction is no mere matter of degree; it is a sharp contrast in *nature.*

6. Man is *capax Dei,* "capable of God." He is constitutionally a God-conscious being. He can know God, respond to him, and commune with him. The lower animals cannot. The most exhaustive animal psychology has never found the faintest hint of either moral awareness or awareness of a Supreme Being. It is almost comical to think of the beasts as having such. This, therefore, is another case of an attri-

116

bute which is either there, or not there. In man it is *there:* in the lower animals, absolutely not.

7. Man alone of all earthly creatures has the faculty of *speech*. That is yet another feature which does not exist in higher or lower degree. It inseparably belongs to man as an adjunct and extension and expression of intellect. The lower animals are simply devoid of it. Its uniqueness in man further corroborates a difference in *nature*.

8. Man has an ineradicable conviction of *responsibility*— of accountability to his Maker and Owner. The lower animals are utterly destitute of any such. For man also there is a declared day of coming judgment, endorsing that sense of responsibility which is native and peculiar to man.

9. In Genesis 3:22 there is another colloquy within the divine Triunity concerning man. "Behold, the man is become as one of us, to know good and evil. . . ." Could any such words ever have been spoken of the beasts? The very absurdity of the idea is complementive confirmation of the deep, wide *difference* between human nature and that of the subordinate creatures.

10. Human beings have *personality:* the lower animals do *not*. Certainly the nonhuman creatures have "individuality." We see it in household pets, farm animals, and in others. Individuality, however, is a far cry from personalness. We would never think of calling our dogs and cats persons! "Personality" may be elusively indefinable, but it is a fundamental phenomenon. God has personality. Satan, the angels, the demons have personality. So do we humans. The beasts do *not,* a fact which marks still another dividing line between human nature and all the lower orders.

If all those ten differentiae together do not proclaim loudly that man is different in *nature* from all the flesh, fish, and fowl over which God gave him dominion, then evidence is useless and logic worthless. Yet Mr. Emmerson says, "Into the creation of man went the same constituent elements that went into the creation of the beast of the field—no more and no less!" How blind can adherence to a theory make us?

All this has its bearing upon the soul-sleep theory, as we shall soon see. Before we come to that, however, there are two or three other factors to mention.

QUOTATIONS FROM ECCLESIASTES

In advocating the basic sameness of man and beast, Mr. Emmerson quotes Ecclesiastes 3:19. It says, "For that which befalleth the sons of men befalleth beasts; even one thing befalleth them: as the one dieth, so dieth the other; yea, they have all one breath; so that a man hath no preeminence above a beast: for all is vanity."

But what about the next verse (v. 20), which says that "all turn to dust again"? That cannot apply to the human *soul*, for the soul neither came from the dust nor can it (being non-physical) "turn to dust." Moreover, when God said to Adam, "Dust thou art, and unto dust shalt thou return" (Gen. 3:19), obviously he meant only the body; for the soul had *not* come from the dust, but from the *breath of God.*

And what about that next verse (v. 21)? It asks, "Who knoweth the spirit of man that goeth *upward,* and the spirit of the beast that goeth *downward* to the earth?" Does not that "upward" versus "downward" indicate a sharp opposite between man and the non-human animals?

Those incidental objections I need not press, for there is a fatal disqualification of quotations from Ecclesiastes which puts them "out of court." Our Seventh-Day Adventists have a conspicuous fondness for quoting Ecclesiastes and Job. A word of caution is appropriate. In most of Ecclesiastes the speaker is not God, but Koheleth. Its opening sentence is, "The words of the preacher [Koheleth]. . . ." I believe in the divine inspiration of the whole Bible. I believe, therefore, that the *record* of what Koheleth says is divinely inspired. But much of what Koheleth surmised was *not,* for he was viewing things from the earthbound standpoint of the merely "natural man." The same is true of Job's comforters, Eliphaz, Bildad, and Zophar, in the Book of Job. Their words must not be quoted as divinely inspired (though they often *are* so quoted), for in the epilogue God himself says to Eliphaz, "My wrath is kindled against thee, and against thy two friends: for ye have not spoken of me the thing that is right . . ." (Job 42:7).

As for Ecclesiastes, it is a *sermon.* Its theme is: What is the chief good? We are meant to see where the quest for the chief good leads when conducted simply on the ground of natural experience, observation, and induction. Then the quest is reviewed in chapters 9 through 12. That is why nearly all Koheleth says is in the past tense: "I said . . . I sought . . . I considered." In all of which he is not stating divine doctrine, but only reporting his earlier quest and interim conclusions. Therefore, when Seventh-Day Adventist brethren quote words like those of Ecclesiastes 3:19 about men and beasts, they are not quoting God, but the mistaken inference of a *man*—a mistaken inference which Koheleth himself later amends (see Ecclesiastes 12:5, 7). Why, then, do Seventh-Day Adventists keep harking back to those several texts in Job and Ecclesiastes and the Psalms while they keep shutting out the fuller light given to us in the New Testament? It is because the New Testament revelation *refutes* their aberrant theories, as we shall presently try to show.

DEATH, SOUL-SLEEP, RESURRECTION

That brings us right to the doorstep of the soul-sleep theory as taught by the Seventh-Day Adventists. Let us quote again their own apostle. His purpose is to show that at death there is not just a *suspension* of consciousness, but a complete cessation of the whole human being. He submits Psalm 146:4, and then characteristically turns again to

Ecclesiastes. As we have shown, however, quotations from that book are not to be taken as "Thus saith Jehovah" when they are only "Thus thought Koheleth." So what of Psalm 146:4? It counsels us not to trust in man for deliverance, because "his breath goeth forth, he returneth to his earth; in that very day his thoughts perish." Yet to argue from that text the extinction of the whole man is extravagant exegesis. A truer translation of its last clause would be, "his *plans* perish" (ERV, ASV, RSV). It does not mean extinction of the *mind!* In any case, the only part of man which can return to the earth (Hebrew: soil or ground) is that which came from it. To claim that this means the outright destruction of the total human person is exegetical malpractice.

And if our Seventh-Day Adventist expositors quote the Psalms, may not *we* do so in reply? The inspired psalmist looks up to God and sings, "Thou shalt guide me with thy counsel, and afterward *receive me to glory.* Whom have I in heaven but thee? And there is none upon earth that I desire beside thee" (Ps. 73:24-25). No thought of soul-sleep there, much less of total extinction! Nor is there the minutest fleck of suggestion that between the being "guided" on earth and then being "received into glory" there is some intervening hiatus of eradication!

What about oft-quoted Psalm 16:10-11? "Thou wilt not leave my *soul* in sheol; neither wilt thou suffer thine Holy One to see corruption. Thou wilt show me the path of life: in thy presence is fullness of joy. . . ." Whether we take those words as referring prophetically to Christ or primarily to David, their testimony concerning death and the Beyond is clear. Mark the distinction between *soul* and *flesh* and between *sheol* and *the grave.* The soul is in sheol, but not left there. The body is in the grave but not allowed to see "corruption." No thought *there* of any soul-and-body obliteration until a far-off resurrection day, nor of a soul without *personality!* Clearly, the inspired Word is telling us that at death the body goes to the grave, and the living soul goes to sheol. (More on sheol later.)

In trying to establish that at bodily death the whole man perishes, Mr. Emmerson further comments on Psalm 146:4, "There is no suggestion . . . that the *ruach* (man's spirit) has acquired personality during its sojourn in the flesh." Yet only four paragraphs later he quotes Ezekiel 18:4, "The soul that sinneth, it shall die," and explains in brackets that the soul is "the *personality,* not merely the body." So, in his first comment, man's spirit has *not* personality, while in his next comment the soul *is* the personality. Such strange complication of spirit, soul, and flesh persuades me that Mr. Emmerson must have been imbibing Edward White's "conditional immortality" treatise, *Life in Christ.*

But the self-contradiction grows worse; for if the soul is the real personality, as Mr. Emmerson says, what of his earlier statement, "The idea that . . . an independent, immortal 'soul' was given to man must also be abandoned"? Such contradictions are fatal to the Adventist theory.

In Mr. Emmerson's words, death is "the complete dissolution" of man's being. In it "man dies *wholly and completely."* Yet all through the Bible there are evidences to the contrary. Go right back to earliest times, to Jacob's lament over Joseph (Gen. 37:35). "I will go down into the grave unto my son mourning." Now Jacob thought Joseph had been "devoured" by some beast (v. 33) and therefore was *not* in a grave. Yet he said, "I will go to my son." Why? Because he knew that the body was not the real Joseph, and that Joseph was still alive even though bodily dead. As a matter of exact translation, what Jacob said was, "I will go to *sheol* to my son." So sheol is not just the grave; it is a reality beyond.

What about that murky episode: King Saul's visit to the witch of Endor? (See 1 Samuel 28.) Whether or not it was the real Samuel who appeared from the other side of the grave I need not discuss here. It is what Samuel or his semblance *said* which concerns us: "The Lord will also deliver Israel with thee into the hand of the Philistines: and tomorrow shalt thou and thy sons be *with me*" (v. 19). That simply cannot mean with Samuel in the grave, for Saul and his sons were never put in graves. Saul's body was decapitated and the rest of it hung on a city wall. Later, all four bodies were burned, and the residue of bones buried beneath a tree. What then did Samuel mean by "tomorrow thou shalt be with me?" There is only one true answer: the bodiless Saul and his sons would be in sheol, their real selves *alive* there.

Other such incidents and statements to the same effect might be quoted from different parts of Scripture, but I forbear. However, I simply must add two or three more animadversions on this most drastic of all the Seventh-Day Adventist tenets, the non-personality of man apart from the body, and man's total destruction when the body dies. Mr. Emmerson quotes with approval G. D. Rosenthal: "Neither reason nor revelation offer us any ground whatever for supposing that the soul without the body is *personal*. . . . It is impossible for us to think of personality without *embodiment*" (italics mine). Similarly J. H. Leckie is quoted: "The idea of a disembodied existence exceeds all that is conceivable." And to those excerpts Mr. Emmerson adds this: "The 'person' exists so long as he is possessed of the body, its organ of expression. Without this *there is no 'person'* " (italics mine).

I must speak with respect and restraint, but frankly to my own mind it is a marvel that such intelligent Bible-lovers as the leaders of Seventh-Day Adventism can profess such a wild diversion from biblical truth. No personality without the body! Has *God* a material body? Has Satan? Have the angels? Have the demons? They are all bodiless spirit-beings. But is God *personal*? Is Satan personal? Are the angels? Are the demons? Of course they are. All are bodiless yet personal. It is the body itself which is non-personal. It is the in-cohering *soul* which is the real human person—as a thousand evidences daily corroborate.

122

A MISLEADING MISNOMER

I think again of Mr. Emmerson's statement: "Death, whether of man or beast, involves a complete *dissolution of being.*" That being so, are we not justified in administering a reproof? If death is such an utter extinction, how misleading it is to call it merely "soul-*sleep*"! From sleep one awakes, but from nonexistence there can be no waking. Our Adventist brethren teach that there will be a resurrection of those who "sleep" in death; but they simply cannot be raised if death is eradication. That is obvious, for if death absolutely destroys a person, there is a sheer blank where that person formerly was; and (I speak reverently) even God cannot resurrect what is nonexistent. He may create a new being *like* the obliterated one, but that is not resurrection. No copy is identical with what it copies. No replica is the same as what it replaces. Even the closest facsimile is not the original.

On such a theory of resurrection, all who stand before the throne of final judgment must be new beings who receive sentence for acts committed by extinct predecessors. And all who receive rewards for Christian service will be new beings who receive them for now-obliterated persons whom they never knew! Such a concept is so evidently a *reductio ad absurdum,* Seventh-Day Adventist leaders would fain modify or soften it, but they cannot avoid it. What do they say about it? Mr. Emmerson tells us:

> If the individual who dies is literally "gone to nothing," what identity can there be between the "person" who dies and the "person" who comes alive through the divine plan of recovery? . . . Admittedly we *cannot fully understand this divine mystery,* just as we are impotent to understand many others.

What an admission! And no wonder; for how *can* they "understand" a mystery which is an absurdity? In reality, it is a confession that the theory lands us in a huge self-contradiction; in a sheer impossibility.

NEW TESTAMENT EVIDENCE

When we turn from the Old Testament to the New we soon find outright refutations of the theory. In Luke 16:19-31 our Lord tells us about the rich man and Lazarus—that after death the former, now bodiless, was in *hades*, alive, fully conscious, and suffering. (Hades is the New Testament equivalent of sheol.) As for Lazarus, he too had gone there, but was in the "Abraham's bosom" part of hades, alive, conscious, and comforted. To any open-minded reader, that is so clearly the *prima facie* meaning, one wonders how Seventh-Day Adventist interpreters get around it. Mr. Emmerson has no comment, so we must turn elsewhere.

Copyrighted in 1966 and issued under assignment from the General Conference of Seventh-Day Adventists, a massive work in two large volumes by Professor Le Roy Edwin Froom was published under the title *The Conditionalist Faith of our Fathers*. A more ably written work one could not desire. It is a standard compendium of Seventh-Day Adventist belief and doctrine. Does it deal with the rich man and Lazarus? It does.

With no disrespect, may I point out some initial blunders? Professor Froom says that the parable is "often cited as the chief cornerstone" in support of man's supposed "inherent immortality" and the supposed "*endless* duration" of the misery which must be endured by the "incorrigibly wicked." He is wrong. Most evangelicals believe that the passage refers only to the interval between death and future resurrection.

Professor Froom further says that the parable depicts the disembodied rich man as "already suffering the tormenting flames of 'hell' "—the final doom of the impenitent. Wrong again. Jesus said the man was only in *hades*, the intermediate internment, not in gehenna.

Next, the professor says that the "common contention

based on this passage" is, that "upon leaving this world all men go at once either into a state of blessed joy or to unchangeable Eternal Torment." Wrong again. Dr. Froom should know better, for he later quotes the explanatory note on this passage in the "Scofield Bible."

He then affirms that this parable is "the only passage in the New Testament in which a person is said to be in *hades.*" Has he forgotten Acts 2:25-31 where Peter says that David had been in hades, and that our Lord Jesus had just come back from there? Has he forgotten 2 Peter 2:4, "God spared not the angels that sinned, but cast them down to Tartarus . . . to be reserved unto judgment"? Dr. Froom himself later admits that Tartarus is beyond the grave and inter-mediate—a "place of temporary confinement" until judgment, and that the fallen angels are there consciously.

And what about 1 Peter 3:18-19? It says (literally trans-lated) that our Lord, "having been put to death in the flesh but having been made alive by the Spirit in which also, having gone to the spirits in prison, he preached [to them]." Those spirits were human beings who had lived on earth "in the days of Noah" (v. 20), and they were now "in-prison spirits." What can that prison be but hades? And what use was our Lord's addressing them if they were unconscious, or rather, "asleep" in the sense of extinction? What does Dr. Froom say to that?

First he says that this passage is "admittedly difficult of interpretation"; to which he adds, "We must beware lest one text be allowed . . . to check the whole central current of consistent Scripture teaching"; which is an admission that it cuts right across their Seventh-Day Adventist theory.

One thing is crystal clear. Those two Greek participle verbs in 1 Peter 3:18, "having been put to death" and "hav-ing been quickened," belong inseparably together; which means that it was immediately after both that our Lord went to those "spirits in prison." Yet Dr. Froom resorts to the artificial Bullinger notion and says, "Since the text says that the preaching was done 'when once the longsuffering of God waited in the days of Noah,' it must be Noah's generation that heard the preaching of Christ through the Spirit." So it was away back in Noah's time that our Lord preached to them; and *after* his preaching, therefore, that they were consigned to the "prison"! Now I put it to any open-minded person: Can we reasonably think that right in the middle of referring to our Lord's death on the cross, Peter suddenly jumps back 2,500 years, to the days before the Flood, meaning that our Lord preached on earth away back then? Surely such misconstruing is quite foreign to the text.

But even if, for argument's sake, we were to allow such to be the meaning, what then? It would only land the Seventh-Day brethren in further contradiction. Those long-ago antediluvians could not have been in the "prison" while they were still on earth and being preached to. So (we repeat for emphasis) they must have gone to that "prison" when they *died:* which of course knocks out the Adventist dictum that bodily death ends all. Furthermore, whether our Lord preached to them in the pre-Flood days, or between his death and resurrection, does not alter this fact, that those people lived on earth, then died, and then went to the "prison," for Peter's words mean that they were the "in-prison" spirits at the time of his writing. So there *is* an intermediate state, a sheol or hades where human spirits are—alive and conscious after death.

So where are we? or rather, where are the soul-death champions? I challenge them to show me anywhere in Scripture that the "*gospel* was preached" (1 Peter 4:6) to those antediluvians while they were on earth. There is not a hint of it in the Genesis narrative, nor in the Hebrews 11:7 flashback. If the Gospel *was* preached to them then, it was an utter failure. Not a soul on earth responded. Not a soul was saved outside the family of Noah. I maintain, then, that Peter's words (when untampered with) clearly mean that our Lord preached to those souls *when* they were

126

in the "prison"—which confirms a post-mortem hades where departed humans are detained between death and the final Judgment Day.

Allow me just one further observation on 1 Peter 3:18, if only to make the meaning finally perspicuous. Mark the sharp contrast made between our Lord's death "in the *flesh*" and his being "*quickened* by the Spirit.*" The next clause, "By which [i.e., in the Spirit] also he went and preached . . . ," is so closely knit to the foregoing clause, it simply must mean that he went and preached to those spirits in hades *then,* between his crucifixion and his resurrection. The whole point of Peter's words is, that *although* our Lord died "in the flesh" his real self was "quickened" for what he then did before his resurrection.

"WRESTING" THE SCRIPTURES

All the preceding reflections stem from Dr. Froom's remark that our Lord's description of the disembodied "rich man" (Luke 16) is "the only passage in the New Testament in which a person is said to be in hades." More might be added on that, but we forbear.

I do not and will not doubt the motives of our Seventh-Day Adventist brethren. I believe them to be honorable men. I am the more grieved, therefore, at the way clear Scriptures have to be discredited or maneuvered by them to fit their theory. Think of it: thirty-five large pages written around our Lord's paragraph about the rich man and Lazarus, all to turn its meaning around! In order to do so, Professor Froom has to *weaken* it bit by bit. To begin with, he denies that our Lord was speaking of real persons: he was only using a "parable." Then he starts explaining that "parables are often based on folklore or fables." After that comes the further explanation that "A fable, or apologue, is a fictitious narrative—a legend, myth . . . a story in which unusual actions are ascribed . . . *which actually could not happen*" (italics his own). Next, and worse, comes this:

"The story of the rich man and Lazarus . . . was really a parabolic fable based on contemporary Pharisaic tradition, but brought from *pagan* backgrounds"!

Where is Dr. Froom taking us? First it is only a parable, then folklore, fable, fictitious narrative, legend, myth in which described actions "actually could not happen"! He next warns us that, "Parables are not a sound basis for doctrine." Then why, may we ask, does Scripture say that our Lord "*taught* by parables"? Some of his greatest teachings were by parables. He used parables to illustrate, vivify, and *confirm* doctrine. That is just what our Lord's account of the rich man and Lazarus does.

But now a further quote. Dr. Froom says, "Here, in the parable of Luke 16:19-31, the unconscious dead are represented as carrying on a conversation—*but without necessarily involving the actual consciousness of the dead*" (italics Dr. Froom's). What a conundrum—dead and utterly unconscious yet conversing with each other!

Alas, there is worse. I quote: "Its personages—the rich man and Lazarus—were not actual historical figures, but imaginary characters representing *classes of people.*" Thus, bit by bit, our Lord's testimony is broken down. But worst of all comes this: "In a parable . . . consistency, reasonableness, or *truthfulness* are not prerequisite"! To me, that seems precariously near to being an irreverent innuendo—a reflection on our divine Lord, though I know it is not meant to be.

But *why* all this weakening, circumventing, and eventually contradicting of Scripture by men who profess to be loyalists to God's Word? As for myself, I could no more treat the Bible in that way than I could tell a lie under oath. To my own mind, this casuistic treatment of our Lord's plain words is pitiful—all to make them fit in with a theory based on a myopic misinterpretation of the "breath of life" by which man became a living soul, and a few tentative observations made by Koheleth in Ecclesiastes along with a quotation or two from Job and the Psalms. Do I need to remind anyone that the Bible is a *developing* revelation?

Why, then, must Seventh-Day Adventists keep interpreting the New Testament subordinately to the Old, instead of interpreting the Old in the much fuller light of the New? Why keep running back to a few twinkling stars in the pre-dawn firmament when the *sun* has arisen?

I cannot give more space here; but what I have said about the Adventists' treatment of our Lord's testimony concerning the rich man and Lazarus is equally true of the way they treat other inconvenient passages. I think, for instance, of the way in which, bit by bit, they divert the meaning of our Lord's gracious reply to the repentant malefactor crucified on the adjacent cross: "Verily I say unto thee, Today shalt thou be with me in paradise." By the time they have filled fifteen pages doctoring the meaning of "paradise," and repunctuating the clauses, etc., the words are given an abstruseness of dispensational content not one bit of which the dying man could have grasped, and as different from what our Lord intended as chalk is different from cheese. However, I add no more about that here, as it will crop up later.

I append only one word more. My mind fairly staggered as I read the Seventh-Day Adventist teaching on the interval between our Lord's death and resurrection. Dr. Froom says, "It is essential to establish the fact that Christ *died* on Calvary—truly *died*. And no inner or real self, or being, *as a separate or continuing entity* lived during the period between his giving up the 'ghost' or 'expiring' and his resurrection on the third day." So the incarnate God the Son not only underwent bodily decease, but he himself, his "real self," became completely extirpated, absolutely non-existent! That is not merely suggested, it is strongly emphasized; and it advertises in a startling way the outrageousness of the Seventh-Day Adventist theory. Through the wondrous mystery of the Incarnation our Lord Jesus was both Son of God and Son of Man, two natures in the one indivisible Person. He was the *God-man*. His absolute deity could not be separated from his perfect humanity. Therefore, to say

129

that *he* became totally obliterated is to teach the extinction of Deity, of the uncreated, eternal Second Person of the triune Godhead! To what wild lengths are men led by obsession with a false theory!

But besides the shock of it is its *absurdity*. Even our Lord's body, let alone his real being, was not allowed to decompose into nonexistence. On the resurrection morn it was the *same* body which was resuscitated; but if our Lord himself had passed into absolute nonexistence it was *not* the same person who "rose." Even God cannot resurrect nothingness. So, according to Dr. Froom, the "resurrection" was only apparent, not real. God must have created a new person—someone other than Jesus. Jesus himself was *not* risen. That resurrection morn was *not* a victory: it was defeat and make-believe. Our Seventh-Day Adventist theorists simply cannot get over that. To "raise" the obliterated is *impossible*.

All kinds of other considerations unite to refute the Adventist theory. Texts all over the New Testament rise up and point their condemning finger at such error. In John 2:19 our Lord says of his physical body, "Destroy this temple, and in three days I will raise it up." But how could he, if he himself had become dead in the sense of *personal extinction?* In John 10:17-18, he says, "I lay down my life . . . I lay it down of myself . . . and I have power to take it again." But how could he have such self-resurrecting power if, when he laid down his life he slid into utter nonexistence? What about John 3:16, ". . . that whosoever believeth in him should *not perish,* but have everlasting life"? How can that resplendent Gospel guarantee be true if, as the Seventh-Day Adventist theory says, *everything* "perishes" at our bodily death? What about John 10:28, where our heavenly Shepherd says, "I give unto them eternal life, and they shall *never* perish"? If that soul-thrilling promise is true, how can we "perish" into nihility—nothingness—when our body dies?

But again, what about John 8:51? Our Savior says, "Verily, verily [double emphasis], I say unto you, If a man keep my saying, he shall *never see death."* What about Romans 8:38-39? "Neither *death* nor life . . . shall be able to separate us from the love of God. . . ." What about Galatians 2:20, "Christ liveth in me?" Does the indwelling Savior perish into nonexistence with each of us as our bodies die? What about 1 John 5:13, "These things have I written unto you that believe on the name of the Son of God; that ye may know that ye have *eternal* life . . ."? How can that life be "eternal" (i.e., never-ending) if when we die physically it is so utterly quenched as to become a vanished flame, a complete *finis?*

And so we might go on and on with other texts, all of which would become mere verbal varnish, empty pledges, meaningless, or worse, if the Seventh-Day Adventist theory were right. Thank God, it is wrong. On every careful test it proves to be unsound. The more we pry it open, the more confirmed we become that the usual evangelical interpretation of Scripture is true to the Word. Moreover, in my judgment, such a doctrine—not merely of soul-*sleep,* but of complete personal destruction at the death of the body, is as miserable as it is exegetically unsound. As we have already complained: it is constructed on inadequate interpretation of man's creation, bolstered by certain texts here and there in the Old Testament. It is a rotten plank which cannot bear weight; a leaky vessel which cannot hold water; a tire with punctures; a house built on a wobbly foundation.

THE BULLINGER VARIATION

There is another version of this soul-sleep doctrine which we ought to confront before we end this present study. Although it is not so radical as the Seventh-Day Adventist form of it, just as definitely it is a deviation from the traditional evangelical belief, and (so I believe) equally erroneous. It is known as the Bullinger theory.

131

It is so named after its modern progenitor, the late Dr. Ethelbert W. Bullinger, a quite remarkable man. I myself am an early riser, but I have to play "second fiddle" to Bullinger, who, I am told, was at his study desk by five o'clock every morning. He was a specialist in Greek and Hebrew, an assiduous student of Scripture, and a prolific author. Unusual in some ways, he was likable in disposition and exemplary in character.

A whole system of peculiar, hyper-dispensational interpretation is associated with his name, and championed by not a few energetic successors. Into that we need not enter here. We are concerned solely with the Bullingerian soul-sleep idea which teaches that at the death of the body, Christian believers—even though they are "born again" and "alive unto God through Christ"—drop into a "sleep" of outright *unconsciousness* until the Second Advent trumpet awakes them to resurrection.

Alas, although so commendable in the ways we have mentioned, Dr. Bullinger is a regrettable example of how biblical texts are often manipulated in order to adjust them to a theory. We shall look now at some of those texts and the way they are handled.

Let me show how he treats Philippians 1:23-24, where Paul says, "For I am in a strait betwixt two, having a desire to depart, and to be with Christ, which is far better. Nevertheless [for me] to abide in the flesh is more needful for *you.*" Dr. Bullinger, in his *Companion Bible* and in his book *How to Enjoy the Bible,* tells us that in verse 23 the words, "to depart, and to be with Christ" refer to our Lord's second coming, and that Paul had three choices in mind: (1) to "abide in the flesh"; (2) to "depart" (die); and (3) to be "with Christ" at his return and the resurrection of the saints. I have looked up the best Greek scholars. Not one of them agrees with that novelty. The Greek infinitive *to analusai,* translated as "to depart," has in itself no reference whatever to the Second Advent of our Lord, neither has the context. On the contrary, three times Paul strikes

132

a contrast between just the *two* alternatives of living or dying. They are the two choices he has in mind. Any supposition that he had a *third* option in view is extraneous. But of course that which gives the knockout to Bullinger's idea is that whereas he says that Paul had a choice between *three,* Paul himself says, "I am in a strait betwixt *two.*" There is not even the dimmest glimmer of suggestion that between the two there is an intervening soul-sleep of unspecified duration.

THE REPENTANT MALEFACTOR

Let me refer now to another text which Dr. Bullinger adroitly repunctuates so as to tie it in with his soul-sleep idea. As you know, one of the malefactors between whom our Lord was crucified, as he heard our Lord's words from the cross, suddenly saw with opened eyes that Jesus was indeed the true Messiah. As a member of the Barabbas insurrectionist movement, fanatically struggling to "bring in the kingdom" by the sword, he doubtless knew plenty about the teachings and miracles and claims of Jesus, and the predictions Jesus had made about the eventual coming of the "kingdom of heaven." Maybe during sneak visits incognito among the crowds he had watched and listened. Suddenly now, as he hangs tortured and dying, he realizes that Pilate's words, fastened above the cross of Jesus, are true: THIS IS JESUS, THE KING OF THE JEWS. And in instantaneous but sincere contrition he pleads, "Lord, remember me when thou comest into thy kingdom" (Luke 23:42). In the next verse our Lord replies, "Verily I say unto thee, Today shalt thou be with me in paradise."

Reflect carefully. Our Lord and that repentant man on the next cross were suspended there suffering intense pain and burning thirst. It was no time to be choosing words with dialectical or theological nicety. Something had to be said which that pain-racked penitent would understand at once and from which he would get immediate comfort. That is just what happened. Our Lord knew that the dying brigand would understand at once what "paradise" was. *All* the Jews knew. "Paradise" was the "Abraham's bosom" part of hades, where all those departed souls who had died in the faith of Abraham awaited together the coming triumph of the promised Messiah. That is where our Lord himself went when he vacated his body and left it a corpse on the cross. His promise to the crucified penitent hanging next to him was that *he*, too, should be there when they both died.

What comfort that gracious reply must have given to that languishing sufferer! Dr. Bullinger, however, has other ideas. He tells us that the punctuation needs altering, so that instead of reading, "Verily I say unto thee," we should read, "Verily I say unto thee *today*," putting the comma after the word *today* instead of after "Verily I say unto *thee*." By that shift, the meaning is switched. Instead of telling the dying man that "today" he would be in paradise, our Lord was only *saying* "today" that in an indefinite, far-off future the expiring sufferer would wake up from soul-sleep to find himself there.

Dr. Bullinger says that the clause, "I say unto thee *today*," was the common Hebrew idiom for emphasizing a solemn statement. He gives forty references, but all are from Deuteronomy. I have looked them all up. Not one has the slightest bearing on our Lord's words to that dying man on Golgotha, nor confirms the so-called "Hebrew idiom."

But let us see whether the suggested repunctuation is right or wrong when compared with more or less parallel texts. I have looked up every occurrence of the Greek word (*semeron*) translated as "today," especially where approximate parallels occur with our Lord's words, "Verily I say unto thee, Today shalt thou be with me in paradise." In Luke 4:21, where he says, "This day is this scripture fulfilled in your ears," did he mean that he was only *saying* it on that day, or that it was being *fulfilled* on that day? In Luke 19:9 we find practically the same form of address by our Lord to Zaccheus as he used to the crucified criminal: "And

Jesus said unto him, This day is salvation come to this house." Did he mean merely that he was *saying* it on that day? or that the *salvation* had come that day? When he later said to Peter, "Verily I say unto thee, This night, before the cock crow, thou shalt deny me thrice," did he mean that he was only *saying* it on that night? or that Peter's *denial* would happen then?

As for the meaning of "paradise," Dr. Bullinger (I speak respectfully) seems to grope around like a man in a London fog. He says that the word is "never" used of "any place" either "above or under the earth." In fact, at present "it does not *exist.*" Apparently he forgets Paul's testimony in 2 Corinthians 12:2-4, that he had been "caught up" to the "third heaven" which he also calls "paradise."

I am grateful for Dr. Bullinger's admission that our Lord went down into hades between his crucifixion and his resurrection, and that he preached there. But when he went there, was he asleep? And were those inmates of hades whom he addressed all fast asleep? The thought conjures up a strangely comical picture. In his parable of the rich man and Lazarus (Luke 16) our Lord not only describes the disembodied "rich man" as *suffering* in hades, but Lazarus as "comforted." It is difficult to see how either of them could have experienced such torment or such comfort if both of them were obliviously asleep.

Were Moses and Elijah asleep when they appeared with our Lord on the Mount of Transfiguration? or had they been asleep up to that point? If so, how did they know what was going on in Palestine, and talk to our Lord about his soon-coming "exodus" which he should accomplish on Calvary?

DOES SLEEP REFER TO SOUL OR BODY?
Perhaps someone asks: What about those texts which actually *speak* of departed Christians as being "asleep," notably 1 Thessalonians 4:13-18? Three times in that paragraph Paul uses the word *sleep* of departed saints. "I would not have

you ignorant, brethren, concerning them that are fallen *asleep*" (v. 13). "Them also which are fallen *asleep* in Jesus" (v. 14). "We which . . . remain unto the coming of the Lord shall not precede them that are fallen *asleep*" (v. 15). Do not such texts support the soul-sleep theory? Our answer is unhesitating.

Not only in Scripture, but widely elsewhere, sleep has been used as a figure of death. That is not surprising, for when a body dies and stiffens into the placidity of *rigor mortis,* it looks like *sleep.* In Scripture, *sleep* is used particularly in connection with the death of the godly. Never, however, is it used of the soul, but only of the *body.* Anyone can look up the Scripture references and verify that. Let me mention two or three of them here.

Daniel 12:2 says, "Many of them that *sleep* in the dust of the earth shall awake." In that verse the word *sleep* simply cannot refer to the soul; for how can the nonmaterial sleep in the dust? The same use of *sleep* to mean the death of the body is seen in John 11. Lazarus of Bethany had died. Our Lord said to the Twelve, "Our friend, Lazarus, *sleepeth.*" Later he said plainly, "Lazarus is *dead.*" Those two clauses are parallel. If then the word *sleepeth* refers to the soul, so also does the parallel word *dead.* But who would say that the *soul* of Lazarus was dead? To clinch the matter: when our Lord "wakened" Lazarus, which part of him was it that he wakened? The soul or the body? If it was the soul, that alone would *never* have brought Lazarus's body out of the tomb. Clearly, the sleeping and the waking referred to the body.

Again, in Acts 13:36, Paul says, "For David, after he had served his own generation . . . fell on sleep . . . and saw corruption." So, if the word *sleep* means the soul, then after David died it was his *soul* which saw "corruption." But who would dare suggest that such was Paul's meaning? Clearly the word *sleep* refers to the body.

Even more conclusive is 1 Corinthians 15:51-53. "We shall not all *sleep,* but we shall all be *changed.*" Which part is it which is to be "changed"? There is not one mention of the *soul* in connection with the coming resurrection. The whole chapter is about the resurrection of the *body*, and the change which *it* will undergo from corruption to incorruption, from dishonor to glory, from weakness to power, from being a "natural" body to being a "spiritual" body, from being in "the image of the earthly" to being in "the image of the heavenly." There is not a breath of suggestion as to any intermediate sleep-interval of the *soul*. To settle the point conclusively, put verses 51 and 53 together. "We shall not all *sleep*, but we shall all be changed . . . for this corruptible [i.e., the *body*] must put on incorruption." Need we add more?

But now go back to that paragraph in 1 Thessalonians 4:13-18, with its three occurrences of the word *sleep*. If we say they refer to the soul, what about verse 16? It says, "For the Lord himself shall descend from heaven with a shout . . . and the *dead* in Christ shall rise first." Would our Bullinger soul-sleep theorists dare to say that the word *dead* refers to the *souls* of departed Christians? Then how can we say that the parallel word *sleep* does? This is another instance in which we have two phrases which correspond to each other—"The asleep in Jesus" (v. 14) and "The dead in Christ" (v. 16).

Yes, they are parallel, and mean the same thing. Like all the other Scripture occurrences of the word *sleep* in relation to death, those three in that Thessalonian passage refer to the *body*.

The Book of Genesis ends with the words, "So Joseph died, being an hundred and ten years old: and they embalmed him, and he was put in a coffin in Egypt." Now when it says that Joseph was put into that coffin, does it mean that the *soul*, the real Joseph, was put there? Not at all. It means only that his *body* was put there. The real Joseph had already gone. Equally so, when Christians are spoken of as "falling asleep in Jesus," the allusion is to the body, not the soul. It is a legitimate and sympathetic euphemism for the death of the body, inasmuch as the body *does* now rest until the trumpet sounds to reanimate it at the Parousia.

DEPARTED BUT FULLY CONSCIOUS

That our departed Christian loved ones are not only alive but conscious and in full possession of their mental faculties is made so clear in New Testament comment that one wonders how it can be disbelieved. Their consciousness is neither extinguished nor diminished by their being now away from the mortal frame in which they lived while here on earth. We must never think that the possession of a physical body is necessary to consciousness. The angels are nonphysical spirit-beings. If now and then they assume some optically visible form, it is only a temporary expedient for the purpose of some communication to men. As to their real nature, they are spirits without bodies: but are they unconscious? The very opposite. Not only do they have consciousness, they have mental powers far greater than those of us human mortals. They think and will and act and love and worship and serve altogether apart from a body. Besides that (do I need remind anyone?) even the greatest being of all, God himself, is an infinite but bodiless Spirit. Does our bodiless Creator have consciousness?

Let me reiterate. Our Christian relatives and friends yonder are very much alive and mentally active. In Revelation 6:9, John says, "When he had opened the fifth seal, I saw under the altar the souls of them that were slain for the word of God and for the testimony which they held. And they cried with a loud voice, saying: How long, O Lord, holy and true, dost thou not judge and avenge our blood on them that dwell on the earth?" Are *they* unconscious? Whatever other questions of interpretation may adhere to that text, nothing could be clearer than that those disembodied martyrs are in that upper world consciously. Admittedly, we are dealing with a vision; but what is the point of such a God-given vision unless it is to vivify a *reality?*

The same is true of Revelation 7:9-17, where John sees that "multitude which no man could number" (v. 9), clothed with white robes, and waving victory palms amid the glory of that heavenly homeland. John is told (v. 14), "These are they which came out of great tribulation, and have washed their robes, and made them white in the blood of the Lamb. Therefore are they before the throne of God, and serve him day and night in his temple." As we have earlier commented, that wonderful scene is not to be limited to a yet-future climax. It represents a gathering up yonder which is going on throughout this present age. And are those raptured saints conscious? Certainly: ecstatically so! Observe moreover that they do not come there after some purgatorial quarantine, or after some protracted anesthesia of soul-sleep. There is an immediate translation from tribulation *here* to consummation *there*. What is more, besides immediate transplantation from here to heaven, there is immediate *transformation* which conditions them for participation in that holy society—as is indicated in those "white robes."

During my twenty years in Edinburgh, Scotland, a treasured friend of mine was the Reverend James Macavoy. He, in turn, was a friend of the late Commander Wolfe Murray of the British Navy. There had been a long friendship of the commander with Dr. Ethelbert W. Bullinger, modern apostle of the dispensationalist form of the soul-sleep fabrication. Commander Murray told my friend James Macavoy that Dr. Bullinger, shortly before his demise, had confided to him that if there was one thing which he deeply regretted it was that he had ever propounded the soul-sleep theory. Further reflection had convinced him that it was wrong. I am sorry that the outstanding scholar-expositor did not live long enough to say so publicly; but that he *did* say so I can well believe on such honest and unprejudiced testimony. I am equally sure that Dr. Bullinger now knows by *experience,* in his disembodied state on the other side of the grave, that the soul-sleep teaching

139

is a bad aberration. I am sure that he is now *consciously* in the enrapturing presence of the dear Savior-King whom he sincerely loved and served on earth.

SEVEN

WHAT ABOUT PURGATORY?

Neither by nature nor by desire am I a controversialist. I suspect a lazy streak in me which, under the guise of Christian tolerance, argues that the best way to defeat error is simply to preach the truth. Martin Luther, albeit, smites me "under the fifth rib" when he avers that any Christian minister who is too busy to fight error betrays the Faith: and my preacher-hero, Spurgeon, spears me when he says that where soul-destroying heresies abound every evangelical minister must be a controversialist.

Most of all, the apostle Paul jolts me when he says, "Though we or an angel from heaven preach any other gospel to you than that which we have preached, let him be accursed." How much refuting of destructive error there is in the New Testament epistles! Even our meek and lowly Master himself had to "enter the lists" and do combat against the religious deceivers of old-time Jewry. What responsibility is ours, then, not only to declare the truth but to *defend* it; not only to preach truth but to denounce error!

In the following chapter I am obliged to draw my New Jerusalem blade, and hope I do so with effectiveness. Even so, let me emphasize that we are fighting *error,* not slashing *men.* Even when we are bluntest against "it" we are still cordial toward "him"; for behind every heresy, the real enemy is that "father of lies," Satan. All human deceivers are themselves first deceived by that greatest deceiver of all.

J. S. B.

If these pages happen to be read by Roman Catholics, this part about purgatory should be of particular interest to them, though what is said is equally meant for others who seek information. On the one hand, those who have been born and bred in Roman Catholicism accept unquestioningly the existence of purgatory. On the other hand, Bible-reading evangelical Christians wonder how anyone can believe such an unbiblical vagary.

Because of the acute separation between the teaching of the Roman church and that of Protestant Christianity concerning purgatory, let me emphasize at the outset that whenever I touch on Roman Catholic doctrine or practice, I always make a sharp distinction between the Roman Catholic church and Roman Catholic *individuals*. Whatever my feelings may be about the politico-religious system itself, known as the Roman Catholic church, I always speak with cordial esteem for sincere Roman Catholic individuals. Our Lord Jesus teaches us to love all men. In line with that, everything I say here is said with genuine friendliness.

Let me ask and answer three questions about purgatory: (1) What is it? (2) Where does the idea come from? (3) Why does the Roman church teach it?

Our first obligation is to let the Church of Rome itself tell us through its own loyal penmen what it teaches about purgatory. In some respects that is not too easy, for there is much difference between its theologians both past and present. Some say the purgatorial fire is physical, others that it is purely mental or spiritual. Many insist that the pains there are solely punitive, others that they are partly purgative. Nor is there agreement, past or present, as to how long the awful sufferings last for any given individual.

On one thing, however, *all* seem agreed. For the average Roman Catholic, the tortures in purgatory are exceedingly severe. Theologians following the dictum of Thomas Aquinas hold that "the least pain of purgatory surpasses the greatest on earth." A more recent Roman Catholic writer calls it "a torment far exceeding all the torments of this world."

SOME CLARIFYING QUOTATIONS

Perhaps the fairest thing I can do is to quote from a couple of Roman Catholic books which seem to present purgatory in as faithful and restrained a way as Pope and cardinals could wish. The first is *Purgatory,* by Martin Jugie, translated from the French by Malachy Gerard Carrol. Here are some paragraphs:

> What we know is no mere guesswork. It comes to us stamped with the infallible teaching authority of the Church. [Note: The appeal is to the Roman Catholic church, not to the Bible, the written Word of God. That is understandable, for purgatory, as we shall see, is nowhere taught in Holy Scripture.]
>
> According to this teaching [of the Church] the soul immediately after death goes to heaven, or to hell, or to Purgatory, according to the nature of its relationship with God at the precise moment of death.
>
> If it [the soul] is in a state of perfect friendship with God, being entirely free from both mortal and venial sin, and having done sufficient penance for sins committed after Baptism, it is immediately admitted to the Beatific Vision . . . known as Heaven. [Note: With such perfection required, how few, if any, go to heaven at death!]

If the soul at death is in a state of enmity with God through having one or more mortal sins unrepented of . . . it is driven away from him and plunged into a state of damnation. This state will be eternal, for after death the soul does not change. . . . The damned soul no longer desires God: it detests Him eternally. . . . This state of damnation is called Hell. [What a strange, unbiblical mix-up *that* is!]

Finally, if at death the soul is in a state of grace and amity with God but is yet unworthy to be admitted to the Beatific Vision—either because of venial sin, unrepented, or the lack of sufficient penance for both mortal and venial sins, or both—it must pass some time, long or short according to the amount of its debt, in an intermediate state. . . . This state is designated in the Latin church since the eleventh century by the word, *Purgatory,* that is, a state or place of purification, of expiation. [Note: The salvation of the soul is thus, supposedly, dependent finally on its own atonement, not solely on our Lord's once-for-all atonement on the cross.]

The author adds that this intermediate purgatory is characterized by "mysterious sufferings . . . proportionate to the number and gravity of sins not sufficiently expiated" on earth. It is a station of "*penance,* where the soul must endure the rigors of chastisements," an exile "full of sorrow." The souls imprisoned there "can do nothing for themselves to sweeten or take away the pains to which they are condemned"; but those awful sufferings can be "alleviated and shortened" by the help of "the Church still on earth."

Let me quote further. "A soul may go to Purgatory for three reasons: (1) on account of venial sins not remitted on earth; (2) on account of vicious inclinations left in the soul; (3) on account of temporal punishment due to every sin committed after Baptism and not sufficiently atoned for during life." (Note: this flatly contradicts the clear biblical teaching that all true Christian believers are forgiven *fully and forever.* More on this later.)

The next quotation reads strangely. "No one goes to Purgatory solely for the second reason [i.e., for *inherent* perversion] since vicious inclinations do not in themselves constitute sins. The majority of theologians hold with St.

Thomas [Aquinas] that such inclinations do not survive the first instant that follows separation of soul and body." (Note: That is a bad fallacy. Mere separation from the body cannot rid the soul of such innate "inclinations." Any such inward renewal, whether in this present life or in the Beyond, is exclusively the work of the Holy Spirit, as the Scriptures make very plain. More later.)

Equally strange is the next quotation. "Contrition breathed by the soul at the moment of death suffices to wipe out the *guilt* of venial sin, but there remains the *expiatory* chastisement *fixed by divine justice*" (italics mine). (Note: the Bible knows nothing of such deathbed "guilt" overhanging the born-again Christian. Nor does it come within a million miles of even faintly suggesting any such postmortem "expiation." It teaches us that infinite and final expiation was made on our behalf by the great Sin-bearer on Calvary, and that *nothing* can be added to it.)

THE PRINCIPAL REASON

What, then, is the principal reason for the supposed existence of purgatory? The following quotation gives the answer. "The principal . . . reason for the existence of Purgatory is the temporal *punishment* due to sins committed after Baptism. . . ." (Note: This is flatly against what Scripture teaches, namely, that the *whole* punishment due to the believer's sins was vicariously borne *fully and forever* by our dear Savior on the cross; so that, as Romans 8:1 says, "There is therefore now *no* condemnation to them which are in Christ Jesus.")

To sum up thus far: Purgatory is not for those who die unrepentant. *They* (says the Roman Catholic church) go straight to endless damnation. Purgatory is for baptized members of that church and is where they (supposedly) endure the torturing fire of *penal* chastisement "fixed by divine justice" so as to complete the full atonement (supposedly) required by their sins. Practically all must go there—popes, cardinals, bishops, priests, laity. For pontiffs, cardinals, and bishops, prayers and masses are offered year after year, long after their death; and the fiery tortures in purgatory are intensely severe.

THE "POOR SOULS" IN PURGATORY

Let me turn now to another Roman Catholic publication. It is *The Poor Souls in Purgatory* by the Right Reverend P. W. Keppler, D. D., Bishop of Rottenburg, adapted into English by Stephen Landolt. I cull from it because it seems about the most moderate and sympathetic book I could find on the subject. It mainly consists of Bishop Keppler's counsels to Roman Catholic clergy.

Moderate though he is, page 63 says, "The Poor Souls [in purgatory] are subject to real penal torments, and these torments are greater than any we can imagine in the light of our own experience." He quotes approvingly Saint Catherine of Genoa: "There are no words, figures, or symbols which can explain the torments of the souls in Purgatory. . . . They suffer such extraordinary pains that no tongue can describe and no mind conceive them unless they are revealed by a special grace of God. Such a spark God by his grace showed to this soul [herself], but I cannot express it with my tongue. . . . No tongue can tell, no mind can comprehend what Purgatory really is. I only see that the pain is as great as in hell"!

We could fill pages with the most lurid descriptions of purgatorial horrors, some of them so extravagant as to suggest (so it seems to me) a sick mentality. Bishop Keppler quotes Bourdaloue: "You ask me what those souls suffer. The answer would be easier if you asked me what they do *not* suffer"! Some of the "visions" seem almost sadistically eager to add more fuel to the burnings in purgatory. Let me give a couple from a book, *Two Ancient Treatises on Purgatory,* by two Jesuit Fathers, republished eighty or ninety years ago:

You must then conceive Purgatory to be a vast, darksome, and hideous chaos, full of fire and flames, in which the souls are kept close prisoners until they have fully satisfied for all their misdemeanors, according to the estimate of Divine Justice. For God has made choice of this element of fire wherewith to punish souls because it is the most active, piercing, sensible and insupportable of all. (p. 131)

Good God, how the great saints and doctors astonish me when they treat of this fire, and of the pain of sense, as they call it! For they peremptorily pronounce that the fire which purges those souls, those both happy and unhappy souls, surpasses all the torments that are to be found in this miserable life of man, or are possible to be invented; for so far they go. Out of which it clearly follows that the furious fits of the stone, or raging gout, the tormenting colic, with all the horrible convulsions of the worst of diseases—nay, though you join racks, gridirons, boiling oils, wild beasts, and a hundred horses drawing several ways and tearing one limb from another, with all the other hellish devices of the most barbarous and cruel tyrants—all this does not reach to the least part of the mildest pains in Purgatory. (p. 135)

There are whole books on such visions and revelations of Roman Catholic "saints." Do those which we have selected seem extreme? The *Catholic Dictionary* cautiously advises us: "It must not be supposed that any weight belongs to legends and speculations which abound in mediaeval chronicles and which often appear in modern books." Yes, many of them *do* appear in "modern books." Also, not a few of those which we have in mind have official approval. Thus, on the one hand, the Roman church declares that its doctrine of purgatory is largely built on "tradition," i.e., on the visions and revelations given to Roman Catholic "saints" of bygone days, yet at the same time, in the words of that dictionary, it warns us against them as having no "weight." Is not that a strange self-contradition?

All sorts of things are said about those "poor souls" in purgatory, their various kinds of sufferings, their behavior, what they ask of us, and so on. Not one word of it is based on authentic knowledge or on the written Word of God.

All is an interweave of imagination, supposition, and sporadic visions. Let Roman Catholic spokesmen give us one single verse of Scripture which tells *anything* about the "poor souls" in their suppositionary purgatory. They cannot. Therefore we reject such repugnant concoctions as unscriptural.

Many would be surprised if I were to quote some of the "visions" from which ideas of purgatory are derived. They are monuments of religious gullibility. Our moderate Bishop Keppler says, "Of more recent descriptions we will quote that of Ven. Ann Catherine Emmerich." This is it: "I saw Purgatory. It seemed to me that I was led to a deep abyss. I saw a large expanse. It is touching to see how the Poor Souls are so sad and quiet . . ." etc. That is one of the milder "visions." Let me add one further word from Bishop Keppler concerning the main *purpose* of purgatory. He says, "St. Bonaventure remarks that . . . the purgatorial sufferings have no longer the character of a means of grace or of a remedy, nor are they meritorious, but are simply *punishments,* penal and *atoning* pains" (italics mine). How utterly contrary to the written Word of God such a quack doctrine is!

WHERE DOES THE DOCTRINE COME FROM?
The doctrine of purgatory certainly is fearful. To me it seems deadly cruel. It is enough to suffocate all present joy in God. I know Roman Catholics who live all their days in dread of it—for they have confided so to me. Underneath the demonstrative outward devotions of many an ardent Roman Catholic is that deep-down scare, as many have later testified. What with penance here and purgatory there, it is a sorry outlook. My heart goes out in unfeigned sympathy to those who have been brought up in such doctrines, and who with ingrained credulity acquiesce in them.

When and where did this purgatory fabrication *originate?* Many Roman Catholics may be surprised to learn that it does *not* come from the Bible. It is neither taught there nor even mentioned; nor is there any text which, even by straining and stretching it, can be made to suggest it. Nor is purgatory a hand-down from earliest Christian "tradition." No such doctrine was known in the church of the first days.

Roman Catholic writers would fain persuade us that belief in purgatory is traceable from the earliest days of Christianity. Well, go back to the earliest date after the death of the apostles. We find it in the *catacombs* around the imperial city of Rome. Eventually, in those immense subterranean burying places, over 4 million niches were filled with dead bodies, and were hermetically closed with stones, many of which bear inscriptions and emblematic markings. Not all of them were Christian, but many thousands of them were. The earliest of those date back to about A.D. 140 or 150, that is, no more than some eighty years after the martyrdom of Paul and Peter.

What do those catacombs tell us? The *Encyclopedia Americana* says that the inscriptions were "simple and brief," as for example: Dionysias in Pace ("Dionysias rest in peace"). Other such were: "In Christ" or "In peace" or "She sleeps in Christ." Most of the dead were buried without coffins, but in various places there are sculptured *sarcophagi* of which the above-quoted encyclopedia says, "The oldest sculptures on the sarcophagi depict the deceased in paradise, in the presence of the Good Shepherd. . . ." (Note: They have gone straight to our Lord in paradise, *not* to some purgatory).

There are also *paintings* in those underground Christian cemeteries. Among them are paintings of the Alpha and Omega, the Good Shepherd, *Agnus Dei* (Lamb of God), the phoenix (symbol of immortality), the anchor (symbol of hope), the raising of Lazarus, also pictures of Jonah and the whale (symbol of coming resurrection), and of Noah in the ark. But there is *not one* pictorial semblance of purgatory anywhere.

In those earliest Christian resting-places there are no crucifixes, no prayers for the dead, no appeals to Paul or

Peter or Mary or saints or martyrs. Such did not appear until much later—many of which were graffiti (scratchings) by visiting pilgrims or refugees. As a matter of historical fact, there is no verifiable emergence of the purgatory idea among Christians until some hundreds of years later, by which time the church at Rome had risen to outstanding influence, partly because of its very position in the capital city of the Roman Empire. Nor was it until still later, in the sixth century, by which time the Roman church had assumed leadership throughout Christendom, that purgatory in the full sense was advocated by Pope Gregory I. After that, the idea developed in definiteness and influence. Yet it was not until another thousand years later, at the Council of Trent (1545-63), that purgatory became an official dogma of the Roman Catholic church. Here is what that council decreed (as given in the Roman Catholic books I have already quoted):

> If anyone says that to every penitent sinner who has received the grace of justification, the sin is to such an extent remitted, and the sentence of eternal punishment to such an extent effaced, that there remains no obligation of temporal punishment to be paid either in this world or the next, that is to say, in Purgatory, before heaven is opened for that soul, let him be anathema [accursed].

The Roman church has hurled more anathemas ("let him be accursed") than any other institution ever known. They have been uttered by the supposed representatives of our "meek and lowly" Lord Jesus who taught us to love all men, even our enemies! The terrible thing about the anathema just quoted is that by implication it curses our Lord Jesus himself, and Paul and Peter and the Bible, for they all teach the Gospel of a complete and eternal remission of sin and guilt through the atoning blood of Calvary, without any need of additional atonement by our own sufferings in an imagined purgatory. In reality, the anathema boomerangs back upon the church which dares to invent and enforce dogmas so contrary to the written Word of God.

SUPPOSED PROOFS

But if, then, purgatory is nowhere taught either in the Old Testament or the New, and cannot be found in the belief of the primitive church, where does the Roman church find supposed justification for it? Does it not have at least *some* validating proofs to offer? It does. It appeals to a solitary text in the Apocrypha, and to a few in the Bible, and to random voices from so-called "tradition." I turn again to Bishop Keppler's book. He has a section: *Proof from Sacred Scripture.* At the outset he cautions priests, "We must not pretend to be able to prove the doctrine of Purgatory conclusively from Holy Scripture." What an admission! I am not surprised that for his first proof text he turns to the Apocrypha.

The apocryphal text he requisitions is in 2 Maccabees. He says of it, "Second Maccabees 12:43-46 is the classical passage in the Old Testament." Note that well. It is the "classic" Roman Catholic proof text. Will it hold? He says it is "in the Old Testament." Wrong! Second Maccabees is not, and never was, in the Old Testament: it is in the *Apocrypha.*

What is the Apocrypha? It is a collection of seventeen compositions by Jewish writers, mainly in Hebrew but some in Greek, its different parts being written at intervals between about 180 and 65 B.C., probably at Alexandria. According to the best scholarship, 2 Maccabees was not written until after 130 B.C., which means that it did not exist until considerably *after* the canon of the Old Testament was completed, fixed, and finalized, and that 2 Maccabees has no place in it.

The Jews *never* accepted the apocryphal writings as divinely inspired or authoritative. Josephus, their famous priest-historian (A.D. 37-97) says, "For we [Jews] have . . . only twenty-two books . . . which are justly believed to be divine. . . . It becomes natural to all Jews immediately from birth to esteem those books to contain divine doctrines and to persist in them, and, if occasion be, willingly to die for them." Those twenty-two are the ones which now appear, regrouped, as the thirty-nine in our Old Testament. Let me repeat: the Apocrypha was *never* a part of the authentic Old Testament canon.

As for our Lord Jesus and Paul and Peter and the others associated with them in the founding of the Christian church, they accepted and sanctioned the Scriptures of that Jewish canon just as it stood—and no other. While they and the other writers of the New Testament repeatedly quote from nearly all the Old Testament books, they never once quote from the Apocrypha.

What say the early "Fathers" of the Christian church? Jerome (c. A.D. 340–420) has been ranked with Ambrose, Augustine, and Gregory the Great as one of the greatest four "Doctors" of the Western church. Although not as outstanding as Augustine in other ways, he was superior in accurate learning, especially in matters Jewish and Hebrew. He was the ablest scholar the ancient Western church could boast. His monumental work was the Latin *Vulgate* which translated the Old and New Testaments into Latin. (By that time Latin had largely superseded Greek as the diplomatic language of Europe.) Earlier translations of the Old Testament into Latin had been made from the *Septuagint* (the translation of the Hebrew Old Testament into Greek), but Jerome went right back to the original Hebrew. His *Vulgate* translation into Latin became and remained the only official Bible of the Roman Catholic church, and was confirmed so by the Council of Trent. The *Douay* Version (i.e., the Roman Catholic Bible in our English tongue) is based upon it.

To Jerome, therefore, all loyal Roman Catholics will listen. So, what does *he* say about the Apocrypha? He rejects it unceremoniously. In fact, he speaks of it contemptuously. Why? Because it obviously contains interpolations, forged

153

prophecies, fables, falsehoods, and anachronisms. As for the other early church Fathers, they are silent or differ among themselves. Is that surprising? Few of them knew anything of Hebrew. They could go no nearer to the original than the Greek translations.

But let Pope Gregory the Great (540-604), some two hundred years after Jerome, tell us what *he* thought of the Apocrypha. He sharply distinguishes between the canonical and the apocryphal. When he cites "Holy Scripture" he always means the acceptedly inspired books of the Bible, never the Apocrypha (as seen in his *Moralia*). When he refers to 1 Maccabees he apologizes for making use of writings which had *no proper authority*. It is just the same with the Venerable Bede in the eighth century, and with Nicolas de Lyra in the fourteenth.

Even the Church of Rome itself officially rejects some books of the Apocrypha as spurious—the First Book of Esdras, the Prayer of Manasses, Third and Fourth Maccabees. Yet it presumed to pronounce "accursed" anyone who would not receive the others as authoritative Scripture! No wonder that among Roman Catholic theologians since then some have had a red face and have tried to soften that harsh Tridentine ruling by calling the apocryphal books "deuterocanonical." Official Rome, however, has never revoked that rash decree—which exalts the legend of Tobit, and the fables (so termed by Jerome) of Bel and the dragon to as high an authority as Moses and the prophets and our Lord Jesus and the apostles!

SECOND MACCABEES

As for 2 Maccabees, which contains that solitary "classic" proof text in favor of purgatory, let me quote from the *Imperial Bible Dictionary*. "In respect of trustworthiness, the Second Book of Maccabees does not take rank with the first. It contradicts the first book, giving a totally different and erroneous account of the death of Antiochus Epiphanes (compare 1 Macc. 6:16 with 2 Macc. 1:14-16 and 9:28), while the statements in the letters [written about happenings in Judea and elsewhere] are inconsistent with those in the body of the work. It is, moreover, in many places at variance with Scripture. . . . The work, in a word, is full of chronological errors, exaggerations, miracles and fables, and is therefore a most unsafe guide." That is the document which contains Rome's "classic" proof text! However, we now turn to it and see what it says.

> Judas exhorted the people to keep themselves from sin, forasmuch as they saw before their eyes the things that came to pass for the sins of those that were slain. And when he had made a gathering throughout the company to the sum of two thousand drachmas of silver, he sent it to Jerusalem to offer a sin-offering, doing therein very well and honestly, in that he was mindful of the resurrection. For if he had not hoped that they who were slain should yet be risen again it had been superfluous and vain to pray for the dead. And also in that he perceived that there was great favour laid up for those who died godly, it was a holy and good thought. Whereupon he made a reconciliation for the dead, that they might be delivered from sin. (2 Maccabees 12:42-46)

Well, there it is. Does it mention purgatory? No. Does it imply purgatory? No. Does it teach prayers for the dead? No. Does it say that the two thousand drachmas in any way delivered the slain idolaters? No. Does it indicate that what Judas did was common practice? No. On the contrary, was it not the abnormality of it which made it outstanding? In view of the unreliability and fictitious elements of 2 Maccabees, did it really happen as reported? To build an elaborate doctrine of purgatory on such an uncertain text is like erecting a tower on a bog. In that same book, 2 Maccabees, chapter 7, we are told of seven brothers and their mother, all tortured slowly to death by Antiochus. All those brothers died *confessedly* in hope of a coming resurrection, but is there the slightest suggestion of passing meanwhile into some such place as purgatory? No, the very opposite.

However, since papal Rome says we are to accept a quotation from the Apocrypha as a "classic" proof text, how can it deny us the right to quote *other* texts from the Apocrypha? I quote here just one, yet it is enough to give the knockout blow to the Roman Catholic church's attempt to make 2 Maccabees 12:42–46 imply the existence of purgatory. I quote Wisdom, chapter 3:1-3.

> But the souls of the righteous are in the hand of God, and there shall *no torment touch them*. In the sight of the unwise they seemed to die; and their departure is taken for misery, and their going from us to be utter destruction, but *they are in peace*. (italics mine)

So, according to clear statement, there is *no* purgatorial "torment" for the genuinely godly. No torment can "touch" them. They are straightway "in the hand of God," and are "at peace."

IS THERE BIBLICAL SUPPORT?

What now of those few texts in the New Testament which are supposed to buttress the idea of a purgatory? The first is Matthew 12:32 (repeated in Mark 3:29 and Luke 12:10). Our Lord Jesus says, "Whosoever speaketh a word against the Son of man, it shall be forgiven him: but whosoever speaketh against the Holy Spirit, it shall not be forgiven him, neither in this world, neither in the world to come." How any suggestion of a purgatory can be espied in those words may well puzzle any of us. However, Bishop Keppler's comment is that our Lord's words "would be unintelligible if no forgiveness of sin were possible in the other world." Yet surely that comment is irrelevant, for both he and other Roman Catholic writers tell us that purgatory is a place of *punishment* for those who are *already* "forgiven." Those who suffer there are not pleading "forgiveness"; they are paying off a "debt" (supposedly).

The fact is that the phrase "neither in the world to come" does not refer to life after death at all. The Greek word translated as "world" is *aion,* which means an *age.* What our Lord really said was, "It shall not be forgiven him, neither in this *age* nor in the coming one." I have just looked up a dozen well-known newer versions of the New Testament, and all but two change the word "world" to "age." Our Lord was not making a distinction between life on earth and life in the Beyond. By the "age to come" he meant the messianic age for which those old-time Pharisees and the Jews in general were keenly looking. Alas, his offer of that messianic kingdom was rejected, first morally in Galilee, then later officially at Jerusalem; but the rejected Messiah-Savior-King will yet return, and the Kingdom Age will then most certainly begin, fulfilling our prayer, "Thy kingdom come." Yes, that is what our Lord meant by the "age to come"; and of course it at once cuts out all possible allusion to any such fantasy as purgatory. The effort to extract any semblance of purgatory from Matthew 12:32 is like trying to squeeze juice out of a stone.

MATTHEW 5:25

The next New Testament text appealed to is Matthew 5:25. Bishop Keppler says of it, "The warning of our Lord to be reconciled to one's adversary when still on the way, lest one should be taken to the judge and cast into prison (Matt. 5:25; Luke 12:58-59) and the words, 'Thou shalt not go out from thence till thou repay the last farthing' have been applied to Purgatory." We observe, kindly, that the earnest Bishop does not say that the words *do* refer to purgatory, but only that they "have been applied" to it. We may well ask, "By whom?" Does he prefer not to say?

I speak with sincere respect, but one could almost blush that such scholarly men can offer such patently artificial suggestions. Our Lord's words no more apply to purgatory than to the man in the moon. Let me quote the text. To make sure that we get the true meaning, I give the King James Version and the New English Version side by side.

Authorized Version	*New English Version*
Agree with thine adversary quickly, whiles thou art in the way with him; lest at any time the adversary deliver thee to the judge, and the judge deliver thee to the officer, and thou be cast into prison. Verily I say unto thee, Thou shalt by no means come out thence, till thou hast paid the uttermost farthing.	If someone sues you, come to terms with him promptly while you are both on your way to court; otherwise he may hand you over to the judge, and the judge to the constable, and you will be put in jail. I tell you, once you are there you will not be let out till you have paid the last farthing.

Every term in the text—sues, court, judge, constable, jail, farthing—belongs to legal proceedings *here on earth*. This text, remember, occurs in the Sermon on the Mount, in which our Lord enunciates the moral standards of the "kingdom of heaven." That promised messianic kingdom, as already mentioned, was at that time keenly awaited by Jewish leaders and people, though their concept of it, alas, was too fleshly. The Sermon on the Mount is our Lord's corrective. When the messianic kingdom comes (he tells them) "the meek . . . shall inherit the earth" (Matt. 5:5), for there will be at last absolutely righteous government; but there will be no relaxing of moral and legal standards. Therefore let others be warned, for there will be firm legal exactions against offenders. Later on, in that same discourse, our Lord teaches his disciples to pray, "Thy kingdom come, thy will be done *on earth* as it is in heaven." All the way through, as plainly as can be, our Lord is telling what is to be *on earth* in the Kingdom Age. For Roman Catholic expositors to suggest that his words in Matthew 5:25 have any subtle hint of purgatory is a remarkable picture of drowning men grasping at straws.

FIRST CORINTHIANS 3:11-15

The next proof text submitted is 1 Corinthians 3:11-15. Here it is in full. Observe particularly the words we have put in italics, and bear in mind that the whole paragraph

158

is about Christian *"ministers"* (v. 5) and their work (vv. 9-10).

> For other foundation can no man lay than that is laid, which is Jesus Christ. Now if any man build upon this foundation gold, silver, precious stones, wood, hay, stubble; every man's *work* shall be made manifest: for *the day* shall declare it, because it [each servant's work] shall be revealed by fire; and the fire shall try every man's *work* of what sort it is. If any man's work abide which he hath built thereupon, he shall receive a *reward*. If any man's *work* shall be burned, he shall suffer loss: but he himself shall be saved; yet so as by fire.

As anyone can see, this passage does *not* refer to the salvation of the soul, much less to a present purgatory, but to Christian "work" and its "reward" (if genuine) on "the day" of our Lord's return. Frankly, I marvel that Bishop Keppler cites it, for he himself admits that it *cannot* support the idea of purgatory. He says, "Exegetically, it is certain that this passage speaks *only* of Christian teachers and their fate on . . . the day of the last Judgment." Yet although he thus admits its *non*-reference to purgatory, he says, "1 Corinthians 3:11 is the classic Purgatorial text of the New Testament"! And to that he adds, "Although, according to Schanz, it offers considerable *difficulty,* that text may with great *probability* be interpreted as referring to Purgatory" (italics mine). Was there ever a stranger mix-up? Any competent Roman Catholic exegete knows, deep down, that the passage has not the faintest suggestion of purgatory.

PHILIPPIANS 2:10
Philippians 2:8-10 is a wonderful passage about our Lord's self-humbling "even the death of the cross," and his subsequent exaltation by the Father to utter supremacy. Verses 9 and 10 say,

> Wherefore God also hath highly exalted him, and given him a name which is above every name: that at the name of Jesus every

knee should bow, of [beings] in heaven, and . . . in earth, and . . . under the earth; and that every tongue should confess that Jesus Christ is Lord, to the glory of God the Father.

Although this is another text submitted as a presumed support for purgatory, it is plain that Bishop Keppler himself does not believe it to be valid, for he says, "It has been asserted [may we ask by whom?] that *inferni* [the infernal spirits who are to bow the knee to Jesus] can only mean the Poor Souls [supposedly in purgatory] because the devils and the reprobates in hell do *not* bend their knees to Jesus." But such a gratuitous assumption is a fiction built on a vacuum. I am glad that Bishop Keppler goes on to concede: "But the point emphasized [by the text] is rather that . . . the whole world of spirits and men, even the evil spirits in hell, must submit to Jesus Christ and render him homage." Good! with that we agree. That is the true meaning—no less and no more.

We may add that if there is one place more than another where Paul would have mentioned purgatory, if it existed, it is in that text, Philippians 2:10. He mentions beings in "heaven" and on "earth" and "under the earth." If there were such a place as purgatory, would he not have said so, to make even clearer that in *every* place the knee must bow to Jesus? There are only the three places—"heaven," "earth," "underworld." Where, then, is purgatory? Is it in heaven? No. Is it on earth? No. Is it in the underworld? No. Is it *anywhere?* No.

FIRST CORINTHIANS 15:29

And now 1 Corinthians 15:29 is presented in support of purgatory. Paul asks the question, "Else what shall they do which are baptized for the dead, if the dead rise not at all? Why are they then baptized for the dead?"

The question seems to imply that some among those long-ago Corinthians were undergoing baptismal immersion on behalf of others who had died before being able to be baptized. Whether such baptisms were few or many, and whether they were on behalf of martyrs or for others suddenly deceased, we do not know. My own persuasion is that such proxy baptisms *were* taking place, at least among those Corinthians. It need not surprise us overmuch. Remember the background of those Corinthians. Vicarious baptisms were a hand down from both Jewish and pagan superstitions.

Paul's question must be related to its local context. That Corinthian church has the unhappy singularity of being the only church to which he says, "Ye are yet carnal" and "babes" (1 Cor. 3:1, 3). It was the most mixed-up of all those primitive churches. There were those in it who were wrong about leaders—some saying "I am of Paul," others "I am of Apollos"; wrong about some moral issues (1:12); wrong about legal matters among Christians (6:1-7); about Christian marriage (7:1-17); about meats offered to idols (8:1-13); and wrong about behavior at the Lord's Table (11:17-34). The apostle relates to all of those in his epistle, but there were other irregularities, too, of which he has to say, "The rest will I set in order when I come" (11:34). Likely, one such was *baptism* (1:14-17).

Therefore we simply dare not say that those baptisms for the departed were right. Does Paul approve them? No. Are they mentioned elsewhere? No. Is there any evidence that they were in general practice? No. Are they taught or recommended anywhere? No. The fact is, they were well-meaning but wrong, being resorted to by those who were as yet "babes" in Christian truth, and who did not have, as we now have, the completed New Testament Scriptures to guide them.

But in any case, where in all this does *purgatory* appear? Is it mentioned anywhere throughout that long resurrection chapter? Not once. On the contrary, even those substitute baptisms are shown to be superfluous. Reflect: the whole of that wonderful chapter, 1 Corinthians 15, is about the coming *bodily* resurrection of Christian believers at the return of Christ. Those Corinthian neophytes who were being baptized for dead brethren were apparently afraid that those departed ones would forfeit participation in the coming consummation: so Paul corrects them by showing that all true believers would have their part in the resurrection at the descent of Christ (vv. 22-23), *including* those who are "fallen asleep" (v. 20). Then he tells them how it would happen: "In a moment, in the twinkling of an eye, at the last trumpet. . . ." Yes, *that* is what those misguided baptisms for the dead had in mind: something which was to happen "in an *instant*"—not some slow release of departed Christians from the pangs of a suppositionary, long, drawn-out purgatory.

Incidentally, I notice that in more recent translations of that twenty-ninth verse about baptisms for the dead, the *punctuation* is altered. The late Dr. E. W. Bullinger alters the punctuation still more, insisting that it should read: "Else what are they doing who are being baptized? [It is] for dead [bodies] if the dead rise not at all. Why are they then being baptized for the dead [i.e., for corpses]?" According to that punctuation, the text does not refer to the departed at all. It means that if there is no coming resurrection, then all those converts to the Christian faith were being baptized only to become corpses in the end. But whichever way we punctuate the verse, neither that text, nor the whole chapter, has any reference to purgatory. To imagine that it does is but another case of hallucination by a mirage.

SECOND TIMOTHY 1:16-18
There are just two other texts offered as possible supports for purgatory. They need detain us only briefly. The first is 2 Timothy 1:16-18, which says,

> The Lord give mercy unto the house of Onesiphorus, for he oft refreshed me, and was not ashamed of my chain: but when he was in Rome, he sought me out very diligently, and found me. The Lord grant unto him that he may find mercy of the Lord in that day. . . .

The Roman Catholic comment is: "It may be accepted as certain that Paul in 2 Timothy 1:16-18 speaks of Onesiphorus as of one departed. To the family he wishes God's blessing, but to him [Onesiphorus] a merciful judgment as a reward for the many acts of charity done by him. This wish is a prayer, and the entire passage furnishes an important instance of Apostolic intercession for a departed soul."

That comment, of course, is a convenient exaggeration. It is disqualified on five counts. (1) That Onesiphorus was dead is not a certainty but a surmise. (2) Paul's words, "May the Lord grant to him" are *not* strictly a "prayer," but only an optative wish. (3) Even that wish was not expressed to God, but to Timothy. (4) That wish made not the faintest reference to Onesiphorus's state between death and coming resurrection. (5) Paul's wish was that our Lord would be specially gracious to Onesiphorus *in that day,* namely, the day of our Lord's return in kingdom splendor. Three times in this epistle Paul speaks of "that day," and each time that is the grand event to which it refers (see 1 Tim. 1:12 and 4:8).

Therefore the Roman Catholic assertion that this "entire passage is an important instance of *Apostolic intercession*" for the dead is an overstraining beyond all reason. Talk about straining after a gnat and swallowing a camel! The plain fact is that in the text there is no reference either to prayers for the dead or to the intermediate state between death and the future resurrection.

REVELATION 5:13

Finally, we are asked to accept Revelation 5:13 as a pointer to purgatory. The Roman Catholic notation on it is: "Apocalypse 5:13 speaks of believing and willing adorers only [when it says] 'And every creature which is in heaven, and on earth, and under the earth . . . I heard all saying: To Him that sitteth on the throne and to the Lamb, benediction and honor and glory and power for ever and ever.'

The creatures 'under the earth' must be sought in *Purgatory.*"

So, as a final eye-opener we are now told that purgatory is "under the earth"—elsewhere spoken of as the abode of demons! If that is so, then Christians in purgatory are farther away from heaven than those living on earth! I forbear further comment on such a far-fetched notion. It is not exposition, but *imposition.*

PURGATORY VERSUS SCRIPTURE

To sum up: Since the existence of purgatory is nowhere taught, or mentioned, or even remotely hinted at in New Testament Scripture, and since the merely human voices or visions of so-called "tradition" have utterly no divine validity, and since the doctrine of purgatory contradicts the clearest New Testament teaching, ought it not to be rejected as the baseless threat of a long-camouflaged fraud? I am thinking carefully and speaking deliberately when I denounce it as an unbiblical and non-Christian invention. There is no use appealing to the early Fathers, for on this matter, as on not a few others, they are discordant; and in any case they are but men, without any such inerrant inspiration as we have in the Bible. Nowhere is there a scintilla of authoritative evidence for purgatory. We have examined the *supposed* evidence for it, and it is just about as strong as the thinnest strand of a spider's web.

Why on earth, then, does the Roman Catholic church keep preaching it? The answer is clear. It is indispensable to the whole scheme of Roman theology. That church has defected from the clear-cut New Testament teaching of eternal forgiveness and complete justification by faith alone in the all-sufficient atonement made by our dear Lord. Although in one breath it agrees that the Calvary atonement is infinite, in the next breath it insists that in order to secure justification we must add (supposed) merit-works of our own! No one, says Rome, dies completely justified in Christ; there is a still-lingering "debt" to be paid off. No one dies completely sanctified in Christ, and ready for heaven; there must be an intermediate baptism of torture to finish off the work. Hence the doctrine of purgatory.

Not only the Protestant Reformers, but the Greek Orthodox church rejected that error. Why? Because it was both fictitious and anti-scriptural. Even the Church of Rome itself did not officially adopt it until the Council of Florence in 1443, and even then it did not become official dogma until the Council of Trent (1545–63). By that time the imposture simply had to have the papal imprimatur on it, stamping it as a necessary ingredient of Rome's apostate theological system, and as a threat to would-be defectors, signed and sealed with a useful "curse" on all who would not accept the big lie as God's truth.

That, verily, is the why and wherefore of purgatory. It is the indispensable appendage to the Roman church's twisted doctrine of the Atonement, of justification, of divine forgiveness, of personal salvation. The real Gospel of the New Testament is that we become eternally saved by grace alone on God's part, and by faith alone on our part, through the once-for-all atonement made on Calvary for us, and by being "born again" of the Holy Spirit. Take the following texts:

> Therefore being justified by faith, we have peace with God through our Lord Jesus Christ. (Rom. 5:1)

Observe: Our justification is said to be by faith alone— without penances, payments, purgatory, or self-works of any sort. Note, too, it says that we already are justified and that we already have peace with God. We give ourselves to "good works" because we *are* saved; not in order to *be* saved.

> While we were yet sinners, Christ died for us. Much more then, being *now* justified by his blood, we shall be saved from wrath through him. (Rom. 5:8-9)

165

Being justified *freely* by his [God's] grace through the redemption that is in Christ Jesus. (Rom. 3:24)

There is therefore now *no* condemnation to those which are in Christ Jesus. . . . (Rom. 8:1)

Those clear-worded declarations of our free, complete justification in Christ, here and now, and forever, were written to the first Christian assembly or "church" in *Rome*. Why does the modern Church of Rome obscure their meaning? But see the following texts, also.

Knowing that a man is *not* justified by works [whether penances or other supposed merit-works] but through faith on Jesus Christ . . . we have believed on Jesus Christ that we might be justified by *faith* on Christ . . . for by works [whether here or in a theoretical Purgatory] shall *no* flesh be justified. (Gal. 2:16)

That completely cuts out all supposedly meritorious self-works, penances, indulgences, works of supererogation, as being *superfluous:* utterly valueless as contributories to justification and salvation. The text reemphasizes that salvation is by faith *alone* on the finished atonement of our Lord. That does not in any way detract from the value and beauty of good deeds *in themselves*—for in Christ we are *called* to such commendable acts; but it cuts them out completely as a means of justification and salvation. Good works come afterwards, as a *product* of salvation, not as a payment toward it.

But let me quote just three more texts, this time on the completeness of our forgiveness and cleansing.

And you . . . hath he [God] quickened together with him [Christ], having *forgiven you all* offences. (Col. 2:13)

For by *grace* are ye saved through *faith;* and that not of yourselves: it is the gift of God: *not* of works. . . . (Eph. 2:8-9)

If we walk in the light, as he [God] is in the light, we have fellowship one with another, and the blood of Jesus Christ his Son cleanseth us from *every* sin. (1 John 1:7)

Listen carefully to this. Those texts and others akin, telling us that we are completely justified, forgiven, saved, and cleansed, became true the moment we became united by simple faith to Christ as our Savior. They are true of us *now;* and they will be just as true of us in that solemn hour when we pass from here to the Beyond. Yes, at the very moment of our transition it will *still* be true that in Christ we are completely justified, eternally forgiven, utterly free from "condemnation," and "cleansed from *every* sin." So, if through the grace of God and the redeeming blood of Jesus, we thus pass over, with no remaining debt to pay, and no sins yet unforgiven, and no stains still to be cleansed away, why any *need* for purgatory? What a contradiction it would be! What a strange insult to the gracious promises given to us in God's Word! No wonder the Bible never hints at such a place! It is the Church of Rome alone which perpetuates such a travesty. For the born-again Christian, as 2 Corinthians 5:8 says, to be "absent from the body" is to be *"present with the Lord"*—not in purgatory, but where he now is in "the heavenlies" (Eph. 1:20).

A FINAL WORD

Even so, there is one question which may still linger in some minds. Although at death true Christian believers are indeed completely justified, forgiven, and cleansed from all stain of guilt, what about their *inward condition,* their sin-infected *nature?* How can they pass immediately, in that state, to "the heavenlies"?

Let me answer by first asking a couple of questions. When those of us who know and possess the Lord Jesus were "converted" to him, what happened? We are always glad to tell. Realizing our need of salvation we opened our hearts to him, and by a simple but vital act of faith, received him as our indwelling Savior. How did he come in? He came in by the Holy Spirit. The Holy Spirit thus imparted to us a new spiritual life. In alternate phrase, we became "born again." Or, strictly rendering the Greek *anothen,* we became born "from above." That new life has been in us ever since. We are "regenerated." This, then, is my question: How did that new life, that regeneration, come to us? Did it come instantaneously, or gradually? It came *instantly.* Once there is life there can be gradual increase of it, but spiritual *birth* is necessarily instantaneous. There are no degrees in death. One is either dead or alive; and the cross-over from death to life *must* be instantaneous. One minute we are spiritually dead: the next minute we are spiritually *alive!*

You will see the bearing of that in a moment; but first a further question. The Bible teaches not only "regeneration" through Christ, but the possibility of an inward *sanctification;* an experiential renewal in the very thought-springs of the mind. The new life which came to us at our conversion as a regenerating *infusion* is now meant to become a sanctifying *suffusion* of our whole moral and spiritual being. Oh, it is a wonderful reality; and many of us know something about it in actual experience. How does it come? It comes by our being "filled with the Holy Spirit" (Eph. 5:18, et al.). When does that filling take place? It takes place at the *moment* of our utter yielding of all that we have and are to our dear Lord. The process to that moment may be (and usually is) gradual. Also there may be (and are) different degrees in our yieldedness, and therefore corresponding degrees in the Holy Spirit's possession of us. But the *complete* yielding, and the *in-filling* by the Spirit, happen in a culminating *moment.* It is instantaneous. Not always in that instant is there some electric sensation or emotional rapture or consciousness of a dynamic inner operation. *That* part often comes a bit later; but it *does* come; and thousands have testified so. Some of the best-known men and women of God have left their witness that *suddenly* they have experienced such an inward renewal to inwrought holiness and fellowship with God as they never thought possible this side of heaven.

Furthermore, as we all know, in times of spiritual revival, when the Holy Spirit has moved mightily, saving thousands, and wonderfully renewing the saints, he has often come suddenly upon men and women, *instantaneously* enlightening their minds, and expanding their grasp of divine truth, and transforming their character in a way which otherwise would have taken years. Let me emphasize it: there has been an *instantaneously* in-wrought change.

What I am getting at is this. If the Holy Spirit can, and does, effect in us that spiritual death-to-life miracle of regeneration in an *instant;* and if he can work that in-wrought renewal to holiness *instantaneously,* as so many have testified; and if, in times of revival, he suddenly comes upon persons and effects *instantaneously* a supernormal mental expansion and spiritual enlightenment, can he not effect a similar yet even more decisive transformation within us *instantaneously* in that moment when we pass from earth into the presence of our Savior-King? Certainly he can; and I most assuredly believe that he *does*.

I am indulging in no mere wishful sentimentalism, and certainly no morbidity, when I say that I am looking forward to what we call "death"; for unless I am self-deceived I already have the anticipatory witness of the Holy Spirit within me that in the moment of my passing he will still be within me, my precious divine regenerator, sanctifier, indweller, renewer, and that he will then *instantaneously* so transform me through and through that I shall be thus conditioned for the sinless society of heaven. For the true Christian, therefore, death is no grim portal to some purgatory, but the God-ordained gate to glory.

I think gratefully again of 2 Corinthians 5:8, "To be absent from the body is to be present with the Lord." What precious guarantee it gives me of translation to heaven, of renewal into holiness, of cloudless fellowship with my adorable Savior-King immediately upon my vacating this mortal body! I think of that, so scriptural, so joy-inspiring, and then in fearful contrast I read the following paragraph from leaflets I picked up recently at a Roman Catholic church in Chicago.

> O gentlest heart of Jesus! ever present in the Blessed Sacrament, ever consumed with burning love for the poor captive souls in Purgatory, have mercy on the soul of Thy servant. Be not severe in Thy judgments, but let some drops of Thy precious Blood fall upon the devouring flames, and do Thou, O merciful Saviour, send Thy angels to conduct him to a place of refreshment, light and peace.
> Amen.

What a morbid, ghastly, utterly unscriptural travesty that is! What varnished hypocrisy, for Roman clergy to be teaching that the "heart of Jesus" is consumed with "burning love" for the "poor, captive souls in Purgatory" when by implication of their own purgatory theory it is Jesus himself, as Judge, who sends them there! And what diseased sentiment it is for them to plead that drops of his blood might fall on those "devouring flames"!

PURGATORY? NO!

To see what a baseless misconception the Roman Catholic figment of purgatory is, one only needs to ask the question: How can any amount of either punitive or corrective suffering fundamentally change what a man constitutionally *is*? Think carefully. No degree of suffering can extinguish that hereditary moral perversity which we have all inherited from Adam. God alone, by the Holy Spirit, can eradicate *that*. We all know that torture can greatly affect a man's behavior and disposition. Proud and insolent criminals or stubborn enemies have been brought to their knees, their spirits broken by thrashings, and have come out of their tortures subdued, afraid ever to do the forbidden thing again. Others have become broken and suppressed but bitter. Others have defied all floggings and have died rather than give in. But whatever their reaction, this remains true: that no amount of such torture can ever change the innate moral *constitution* of the man himself, either here or hereafter.

Turn to the last book of the Bible and see *there* whether tortures change men. Revelation 9:17 tells of awful plagues which slay a third part of men and torture the remainder, but do those who endure them change? Verse 21 says, "Neither repented they of their murders, nor of their sorceries. . . ." Chapter 16:9-11 tells of men being "scorched with great heat" and gnawing "their tongues for pain," but does it change them from badness to goodness? On the contrary, verse 11 says, "And [they] blasphemed the God of heaven because of their pains and their sores, and repented not. . . ."

We may take it as axiomatic that torture in itself is powerless to change what we hereditarily *are*. Many of us who have sought to live a life of holiness have had to learn, sometimes by painful frustrations, that self cannot change self. We may discipline ourselves, religionize ourselves, chain, thrash, suppress, or cloister ourselves, but we simply cannot inwardly change ourselves *by* ourselves. Any radical change within us, in our *innate* impulses and propensities, must be effected by a power from outside of us—a *divine* power, namely, the Holy Spirit. That is true whether we are here on earth, or with our Lord in the Beyond, or in some imagined purgatory. Let it be learned once-for-all and forever: Even if there were a purgatory (which there is not) it could *never* change what we fundamentally are. It could *never* miraculously transform us into sinless beings, perfected to enter the "inheritance of the saints in light" (Col. 1:12). The Holy Spirit *alone* can do that. Nor can the enduring of any supposed purgatorial torments *ever* add one mite to the eternally full and final atonement which the dear Son of God made for us on Calvary.

Away then with this unscriptural, *anti*-scriptural doctrine of purgatory. *None* of us will ever go there. It is a *lie*—one of the biggest lies the devil ever palmed off on credulous clerics, and, through them, on unenlightened millions. And let all of us who are born-again Christians sing again with Paul: "To be absent from the body is to be *present with the Lord.*"

EIGHT

SHEOL, HADES, RESURRECTION

In the King James Version of the Bible (often called the Authorized Version) the Hebrew word *sheol* is translated sometimes as "grave," sometimes as "hell," three times as "pit." That inconsistency is unfortunate. Often where the word *grave* occurs, the Hebrew word is a different one from *sheol,* and the average reader cannot know *which* Hebrew word is used. The American Standard Version (ASV) and the Revised Standard Version (RSV) have corrected that fault. Wherever the word is *sheol* in the Hebrew, they have uniformly given it as *sheol* in the English. But whichever version we use, it is helpful to have a list of all the texts in which *sheol* occurs.

Genesis	37:35	Psalms	18:5	Ecclesiastes	9:10
	42:38		30:3	Song of Solomon	8:6
	44:29		31:17	Isaiah	5:14
	44:31		49:14		14:9
Numbers	16:30		49:15		14:11
	16:33		55:15		14:15
Deuteronomy	32:22		86:13		28:15
1 Samuel	2:6		88:3		28:18
2 Samuel	22:6		89:48		38:10
1 Kings	2:6		116:3		38:18
	2:9		139:8		57:9
Job	7:9		141:7	Ezekiel	31:15
	11:8	Proverbs	1:12		31:16
	14:13		5:5		31:17
	17:13		7:27		32:21
	17:16		9:18		32:27
	21:13		15:11	Hosea	13:14
	24:19		15:24	Amos	9:2
	26:6		23:14	Jonah	2:2
Psalms	6:5		27:20	Habbakuk	2:5
	9:17		30:16		
	16:10				

Earlier in these studies we briefly commented on the use of the word *sheol* in the Old Testament. As there is no little divergence of interpretation, however, perhaps there is need for amplified comment here.

In our interpretation of Holy Scripture there are two opposite faults against which we should always be on guard. One is our imaginatively seeing what is not really there. The other is a mechanical dullness to what really *is* there. So far as *sheol* is concerned, there are those who, in my judgment, make the Old Testament references mean more than is strictly allowable, but there are far more who seem bent on disallowing their full force.

Let me make a further preliminary observation. It is fashionable among certain modern scholars to aver that the teachings of the Bible are much flavored by influences from outside. They tell us that in the Old Testament, Hebrew thought about God and the Beyond is considerably shaped by Babylonian and Egyptian ideas; while Christian doctrine in the New Testament is much colored by Greek, Platonic, and other contemporary concepts.

Nothing of the kind! What we have in both Old and New Testaments is not human "thought" but divine *truth*.

175

The inerrantly inspired teachings of the Bible are no more indebted to "external influences" than the light of the sun is indebted to the reflected light of the planets. Granted, in inspiring "holy men of old," the Holy Spirit caused them to use current form and phrase, else the divine communications would not have been readily intelligible; but the revealed truth *itself* is utterly independent of all merely human influence.

OLD TESTAMENT RETICENCE

The first notable feature about Old Testament reference to the Beyond is its *restraint*. That at once marks its independence of outside influences. There is nothing in it of Babylonian, Persian, or Egyptian extravagances or peculiarities. It leaves us wishing it had said more, and longing for that further light which comes to us in the New Testament.

This reticence of the Old Testament is impressive. It is as much an indication of supernatural inspiration as what is revealed. The Bible is almost as remarkable in its reservations as in its revelations. Enough is revealed to make faith intelligent. Enough is reserved to give faith scope for development. If it should be asked *why* there was not fuller Old Testament disclosure concerning the Beyond, the answer is that there could not be larger unveiling until, in the "fullness of the time," God the Son became incarnate, crucified, resurrected, bringing "life and immortality to light through the gospel" (2 Tim. 1:10). Let us thank God for the reserve and *sanity* of the Old Testament, both of which preserve us from eccentric nonbiblical errors and prepare us for the completive truth unloosed to us in the New Testament.

Let this be grasped at once. The Old Testament knows nothing of *extinction*—the idea that when the body dies the human soul also is extinguished. The few texts in Job and Ecclesiastes which superficially could seem to look that way are found on closer inspection to refer only to the body. The teaching of a coming resurrection, and the warnings of a coming Judgment Day, all imply that the departed are still alive. So do instances of persons brought back from death. So, too, the fact that both the Law and Prophets forbid necromancy—conjuring up the spirits of the dead—indicates the general belief in living spirits beyond the grave.

Nor does the Old Testament know anything of *absorption,* the idea that the soul, although it survives the death of the body, eventually loses all individual identity by absorption into the so-called Universal Spirit. Nor does the Old Testament give the slightest foothold to *preexistence,* although belief in the preexistence of souls was widespread, being found even in the Apocrypha and later in the Jewish Talmud. Nor does the Old Testament give even the faintest toleration to the idea of *transmigration.* On the contrary, every human soul is as uniquely new as was Adam, the first man, and David, and Jeremiah (Gen. 2:7; Psalm 139:14-16; Jer. 1:5). The Egyptian *Book of the Dead* bears witness to the wide prevalence of the transmigration theory in Old Testament times, but the Law and the Prophets and the writings of the authentic Hebrew Scriptures have not a fleck of endorsement for it.

This Old Testament moderation, this freedom from all suggestion of extinction, absorption, preexistence, metempsychosis, should be gratefully noted. Had the Scripture penmen been tapping Babylonian, Persian, or Egyptian mythological sources they would have been at no loss for colorful details of sheol and its denizens. Those human spokesmen of Jehovah were held by a sacred restriction. No rein is given to imagination. They speak only as moved by the Holy Spirit. At *their* stage of divine revelation the life hereafter is divulged more in its negative aspects, and with the emphasis on sheol as the place where all *earthly* works, knowledge, and devices come to an end. To elucidate the *positive* aspects of the hereafter, further revelation was needed, which, thank God, came later. What I am stressing is that in the Old Testament, so far as reference

177

to the Beyond is concerned, divine revelation is seen not so much in the degree of the information it gives us as in the way it guards us from error.

Nevertheless, having made that clear, let me at once add that there is also no little enlightening comment, as we shall see, and which we ought to explore. There is a wise maxim which all Bible teachers should heed: Never interpret a text apart from its context, but always in harmony with it. In line with that, all Old Testament references to sheol should be interpreted in accord with the overall Old Testament teaching about *God* and *man*. It is that which separates the Old Testament from all the nonbiblical religions, and gives all its disclosures about a future life their special significance.

In deep, wide divergence from all other deities, Israel worshiped *one God alone,* the Creator of sun, moon, stars, and all other existing realities, including angels and men: invisible, absolutely sovereign, utterly holy, inexorably righteous, yet crowningly a God of compassion who enters into covenant with men and reveals himself as the faithful Creator seeking fellowship with his people; a God to be feared yet loved; infinitely distant in his incomprehensibleness yet exquisitely near in his fatherly warmth. Because Jehovah could not be physically seen, nor was represented by an idol, the polytheistic nations mistook Israel's faith for a religion without a god. Yet it was in his invisible everywhere-presence that he drew near to men, seeking their worship, obedience, and fellowship.

Could such a God have made man just to kill him? Did the grave end all? Or did it denude man of everything worth existing for? Could the shelter of God's wings, to which he invited men, be the place where human life was quenched after so short a flicker, or where the human spirit became no more than a ghost in a shadowy maze? Could his relationship of love and companionship and good purpose be restricted to man's short spell of mortal breath on earth?

Likewise, the Old Testament view of *man* forbids such a conclusion. Those Hebrew Scriptures do not propound a *philosophy* of man. Their concern is exclusively man's relationship to *God;* not what man is in himself, but rather what he means to his Maker. Nowhere does the Old Testament say that God made man immortal, yet neither does it say that man was made constitutionally mortal. What it *does* convey is that man was made for fellowship with God, and that before the Fall, God and man enjoyed such fellowship, and that it would have continued without hint of death if man's disobedience had not broken it. Along with that, man is contrasted with the lower animals. He has a unique relationship with God. He was not meant to die as he now does. He was meant to live; and although he is now fallen, there is God-given hope of restoration. In the religions outside Israel, death is viewed simply as a natural necessity, whereas in the Old Testament death is a *tragedy* due to sin. All the religions outside Israel had their various gods of sheol—the Babylonians their Allat, the Greeks their Pluto and Persephone—but in the Old Testament there is only the one infinite God who fills all the heavens and the earth and is also the righteous One who rules even in sheol; so that Job can say, "Sheol is naked before him" (Job 26:6); and David can say, "If I ascend up into heaven, thou art there: if I make my bed in [sheol], behold, thou art there" (Ps. 139:8). Finally, whatever sheol may be, this one-and-only true God will bring all men out of it eventually for final judgment and an absolutely righteous verdict which then decides their destiny. And however gloomy sheol may seem from the earthward side, it cannot be all dark since the presence of that one true God penetrates even there.

OLD TESTAMENT DATA

With the foregoing considerations in mind, let us now set out the Old Testament data. The word *sheol* occurs 65 times. In our King James Version it is translated "grave"

31 times, "hell" 31 times, and "pit" 3 times. Unfortunately, those words obscure its meaning. It would have been better to bring over into English the actual word "sheol" in each text. That indeed is what the American Standard Version and the Revised Standard Version have done, which greatly helps. At the beginning of this chapter we have listed all the texts where the word occurs. When we dig into those we find that certain features stand out clearly.

1. In all 65 occurences, sheol is not once used in the plural. That is because, as earlier pointed out, sheol does not mean merely the grave. There are not two or three or more sheols, but the one only. Instead of meaning the grave, the very word *sheol* is used to distinguish it from the grave.

2. Nowhere in all those 65 references is there any suggestion that the *body* goes to sheol. The body goes to the grave *(qeber)*, but the soul to sheol.

3. Nor is sheol ever spoken of as being in the ground, or on the surface of the earth, as the grave *(qeber)* is.

4. Nor in all those 65 texts do we find that *man* ever puts anyone into sheol, as he puts bodies into graves.

5. Sheol is never spoken of as digged by man, or owned by man, or even touched by man; whereas men *do* dig and own and touch graves.

6. When the Jews of Old Testament times meant only the grave they used a different word, *qeber*, which occurs 64 times in the Old Testament. It occurs in the plural 29 times. Dead bodies are said to be laid there, 37 times. It is said to be in the earth or ground, 32 times; also to be owned by a man, 44 times; and to have been digged or touched by men, 11 times. So let us grasp this once for all: *qeber* is the grave; *sheol* is the other side of it.

TEMPORARY ABODE OF SOULS

Not only does the Old Testament make indubitably clear the difference between the grave and sheol, it makes equally clear that living souls really *do* go to sheol. In an earlier chapter we examined the theory that at the death of the body the whole human person ceases to exist. Well, here is a big fact which finally disproves that. The Hebrew word for the soul is *nephesh*. It appears over 700 times in the Old Testament, translated by over 40 English words, but mainly by our word *soul* (467 times); and sometimes by the pronoun "he" obviously meaning the real human self or person. Mark this: out of all that number, the Old Testament never once speaks of the *nephesh,* or soul, as going to the grave *(qeber),* but it repeatedly speaks of souls going to *sheol*. If that does not show clearly that the soul and body become separated at the decease of the body, and that the soul departs into the Beyond, I know not what could. The Old Testament rings clear: when we part from life on earth it is the soul, the spirit, the real person which passes into sheol (hades), while the body is interred, burned, or otherwise disintegrated. Nowhere, however, does the Old Testament teach that sheol is the place of *final* human destiny; it conveys, in passages to be cited later, that sheol, although seeming long to human reckoning, is intermediate and temporary.

EVIDENCE OF CONSCIOUSNESS

Among the sheol texts there are those which verify that it is a place of *consciousness*. We read about the "pains of sheol" (Ps. 116:3). There can be no such without consciousness. Isaiah 14:10 tells how the inhabitants of sheol were "stirred" to meet the now-disembodied emperor of Babylon as he came to join them there. That would be strange if they were unconscious. They say to the disrobed new arrival, "Art thou also become weak as we are? Art thou become like unto us?" So there is *speech* in sheol, even though not by tongue or lips. And we are further told, "They [in sheol] that see thee shall *gaze* at thee. . . . Is this the man that made the earth to tremble?" So they *see* each other there, not optically as on earth, but with a soul-faculty of vision which we shall all know when we pass over. How could they thus see if unconscious? Those human spirits in sheol also jibe the now-enfeebled monarch that whereas *their* bodies were now reposing in earthly graves, *his* body is "cast out of thy grave like an abominable branch," and without "burial." Incidentally, note there the distinction made between soul and body, and between grave and sheol.

There is also a striking passage in Ezekiel 32:21-27 where God says of Pharaoh, "The strong among the mighty shall speak to him out of the midst of [sheol]. . . ." Again, "There [in sheol] is Assyria and all her company. . . . There is Elam and all her multitude. . . . There is Meshech, Tubal, . . ." et cetera. What a meeting place! What a tarrying place! What a leveling place! There are no class distinctions there, no social strata of higher and lower, no aristocracy above commonalty, no capitalist versus communist! What does any of that mean there? How many millions are there—not dead, but living!—not asleep, but wide awake!

Of course, it is in the light of the New Testament that many of those Old Testament references to sheol and the after-life flash with fuller meaning. We recall our Lord's answer to the Sadducees in which he reminded them of God's words to Moses from the burning bush of Horeb: "I am the God of Abraham, and the God of Isaac, and the God of Jacob." Our Lord's comment suddenly highlights the special implication of those words. He says, "God is not the God of the dead, but of the *living!*" At the time of the burning bush the bodies of those three patriarchs had been buried for between 150 and 350 years; but had their souls perished with their bodies? or were they fast asleep in sheol? No, they were "living" and conscious.

SHEOL NOT ULTIMATE BUT TEMPORARY

Also, without our needing to overpress the meaning of words, we see Old Testament indications (as noted above) that sheol is not man's ultimate destiny, but *intermediate* and provisional. In Psalm 16:10-11, David is speaking not only prophetically of our Lord's resurrection but of his own hope: "Thou wilt not leave my soul in [sheol]. . . . Thou wilt show me the path of life: in thy presence is fulness of joy. . . ." The same confidence rings out again in Psalm 49:15, "But God will redeem my soul from the power of [sheol]; for he shall receive me." And loudest of all comes God's own promise in Hosea 13:14, "I will ransom them from the power of [sheol]; I will redeem them from death. . . ."

Tied in with that is the Old Testament witness to a coming *Judgment Day*. When the psalmist says, "Therefore the ungodly shall not stand in *the* judgment" (Ps. 1:5), he is thinking, not of any mere earthly judgment by men, but of a final judgment by God. Patriarch Job, in his suffering and bewilderment, foresaw that coming Judgment Day and was comforted by it when he exclaimed, "I know that my Redeemer liveth, and that he shall stand at the latter day upon the earth . . . whom I shall see for myself [or 'on my side,' i.e., as my vindicator] . . . there is a *judgment*" (Job 19:25-29). Implicit also in Job's words, "in my flesh shall I see God" (v. 26), is the apparent anticipation of bodily resurrection; and (observe) the Judgment is *then*.

In keeping with that is Koheleth's conclusion at the end of Ecclesiastes: "For God shall bring every work into judgment, with every secret thing [or, as the Septuagint renders it, 'everything that has been overlooked'], whether it be good, or whether it be evil."

Clearest of all is Daniel's vision: "I beheld till the thrones were cast down [or set] and the Ancient of days did sit, whose garment was white as snow, and the hair of his head like the pure wool: his throne was like the fiery flame, and his wheels as burning fire. A fiery stream issued and came forth from before him: thousands of thousands ministered unto him, and ten thousand times ten thousand stood before him [lit. 'rise up,' in implied resurrection]: the judgment [or the Judge] was set, and the books were opened" (Dan. 7:9-10).

Sheol, then, as we have said, is the internment intervening between the death of the body and that future Judgment Day. All such Old Testament intimations concerning sheol, resurrection, and final judgment are in anticipative accord with the fuller teachings of the New Testament.

DISTINCTIONS IN SHEOL

That there will be fateful distinctions made on the final Judgment Day, between the good and the bad, between the godly and the ungodly, is stated or implied again and again in the Old Testament; but are there such distinctions made beforehand in *sheol* between the upright and the evildoer? Job avers, "Drought and heat consume the snow waters; so doth [sheol] those which have sinned" (Job 24:19). Psalm 9:17 warns, "The wicked shall be turned into [sheol]." Psalm 31:17 adds, "Let the wicked be ashamed, and let them be silent in [sheol]." Psalm 55:15 says, "Let them go down alive into [sheol], for wickedness is in their dwellings." Seemingly, therefore, sheol is a place where the evildoers are stripped of power and imprisoned. It goes ill with them there, hence the poetic parallel in Solomon's Song,

> Love is strong as death; jealousy is cruel [hard] as [sheol]. (Song of Sol. 8:6)

With the godly and upright it is different. *God* is with them in sheol as says the strophe in Psalm 139:8, "If I make my bed in [sheol], behold, thou art there." Sheol may shut the godly off from earth, but it does not shut them off from God. Furthermore, the godly there have hope of eventual emergence, as we see in Psalm 49:15, "God will redeem my soul from the power of [sheol], for he shall receive me"; that is, as he took Enoch to be with himself, so will he take me (the psalmist) to share his heavenly home of rest and joy along with other redeemed ones. That will be "in the morning" (see verse 14); that is, the resurrection morning. Even though disembodied, the godly in sheol can sing the words of Psalm 16:9, "My flesh also shall rest in hope" (i.e., of resurrection).

So, then, although for the evildoer sheol is an unrelieved gloom, the godly there have the sustaining presence of God and a bright light shining ahead. They are "prisoners of *hope*" (Zech. 9:12). That hope gleams in other passages besides those already quoted. In their bearing on this, quite remarkable are the words of Zechariah 9:9-17 about the coming of Messiah-King and the final deliverance of Jerusalem. In verse 11 God says, "Because of the blood of thy covenant [i.e., God's blood-sealed covenant with Israel] I do set free thy prisoners. . . . Turn ye to the stronghold ye prisoners of hope." It is notable that in the Hebrew the word *hope* has the article—which elsewhere it does not. It is "*the* hope of Israel" distinctively (see Acts 26:6-8); namely, the coming of Messiah and the resurrection of Israel's godly dead. That Messianic hope and the liberating of the godly from sheol belonged together. Is there not another allusion to that in the Messianic prophecy of Isaiah 42? "I, Jehovah, have called thee [the coming Messiah] . . . to bring out the prisoners from the dungeon, and them that sit in darkness in the prison-house." Is there not another latent echo of it in Isaiah 49:9?

Admittedly, the distinctions between the godly and the ungodly in sheol are not made as sharply in Old Testament statement as in the New, but they are there. They are implied also in the distinction made between the upright and the wicked in the coming resurrection and judgment, emphatically so in Daniel 12:2, "Many of them that sleep in the dust of the earth shall awake, some to everlasting life, and some to shame and everlasting contempt."

WHERE IS SHEOL?

Can we know *where* sheol is? Perhaps we ought first to learn where it is *not*. It certainly catches the eye that in the 65 places where the word *sheol* occurs, no less than 29 speak of it as "down." Its first occurrence, for example (Gen. 37:35), is quite definite: "I will go *down* to sheol mourning." Similarly in Isaiah 14:9 we read, "Sheol from *beneath* is moved for thee, to meet thee at thy coming."

On that basis, along with certain other Scriptures, some earnest brethren maintain that sheol is actually under the ground, deep in the physical earth. They are so sincere, so conscientiously determined to keep literally to the written Word, that one hesitates to criticize; yet I believe they are wrong. Their proof texts are the following, especially the italicized phrases.

> But those that seek my soul, to destroy it, shall go into the *lower parts of the earth*. (Ps. 63:9)
>
> They are all delivered unto death, to the *nether [lower] parts of the earth* . . . with them that go down to the pit. (Ezek. 31:14)
>
> Cast them [multitude of Egypt] down . . . unto the *nether parts of the earth*. . . . (Ezek. 32:18)
>
> Elam and all her multitude . . . are gone down . . . into the *nether parts of the earth* . . . with them that go down to the pit. (Ezek. 32:24)

That phrase, "the lower parts of the earth," is supposed to show that sheol is deep inside the earth; and those who teach so link it with our Lord's words in Matthew 12:40, "As Jonas was three days and three nights in the whale's belly; so shall the Son of man be three days and three nights in the heart of the *earth*." They also quote Ephesians 4:9, "He who ascended [our Lord Jesus] . . . descended first into the lower parts of the earth." And of course there is Philippians 2:10, which tells us that "at the name of Jesus every knee should bow, of [beings] in heaven, and . . . on earth, and . . . *under the earth*." Revelation 5:3 and 13 are to the same effect.

Yet there are cogent objections to such an inference. A sound principle in interpreting the Bible is that wherever it can reasonably be taken literally, it should be so taken.

The meaning which seems most natural should be regarded as the *true* meaning. Yet it is also true that the Bible does use popular phrases sometimes in a figurative way, and rightly so. That pertains, so I believe, to the expression, "the lower parts of the earth."

Before I quote Scripture texts against an underground sheol, let me register what I think may be called a common-sense objection to it. I cannot see how a vast cavern somewhere deep inside the physical earth could confine nonphysical, disembodied human *spirits*. If this revolving physical orb *could* imprison purely spiritual beings, then contradictorily enough it would burn them to nothingness by the intense internal fire which becomes increasingly hotter toward its center. From evidence furnished by volcanoes, thermal springs, and deep mine shafts, the temperature increase is about one degree Fahrenheit for every sixty feet of descent. A depth of two miles would be as hot as boiling water, and at fifty miles deep the heat would be such as would melt every known solid. I can hardly think that our Lord went *there* between his crucifixion and resurrection.

There are also scriptural reasons for rejecting the idea that the phrase "lower parts of the earth" means *inside* the earth or under the ground. In Psalm 139:15, where David refers to the wonder of human birth, he says, "My frame was not hidden from thee when I was made in secret and curiously wrought in the lowest parts of the earth." When David thus referred to his prenatal formation in the womb he certainly did not mean under the ground, or, to use a common expression, "the bowels of the earth." His phrase is *not* to be taken literally.

Similarly, in Isaiah 44:23, where the prophet exclaims, "Sing, O ye heavens, for Jehovah hath done it: shout, ye *lower parts of the earth,*" he does not mean somewhere below the ground, or an underworld. Like David, he is simply making a contrast between heaven high above and earth low beneath.

Even in Ezekiel 31:15-18, which is claimed as favoring

the notion that sheol is somewhere beneath the earth's crust, we find that the phrase "nether parts of the earth" is used, *not* of under the earth, but *on* it. God says, "I made the nations to shake at the sound of his [Assyria's] fall, when I cast him down to [sheol] . . . and . . . all that drink water, were comforted in the *nether parts of the earth.*" Plainly, those who "drink water" are on earth, not under it.

Likewise, when our Lord said that he would be three days and three nights "in the heart of the earth" the wording was surely meant to be taken figuratively. He drew a parallel with Jonah: "As Jonas was three days and three nights in the whale's belly . . ." But Jonah's own comment was, "Out of the belly of *sheol* cried I." Did he mean, then, that sheol was actually in the interior of the sea-monster? No. His words are to be taken figuratively. In order to avoid admitting this, there are some who tell us that Jonah actually died and rose again. I quote: "Jonah was truly dead and raised again." Supposedly, his body remained in the fish while he himself went down into sheol, after which his soul rejoined his body and thus he was resurrected. But that is seeing what is not there. The Scripture reads clear: "Jonah was in the belly of the fish three days and three nights" (Jonah 1:17). Moreover the "sheol" from which he prayed was also the inside of the fish, for Jonah 2:1-2 says, "Jonah prayed unto Jehovah his God out of the fish's belly. . . . Out of the belly of *[sheol]* cried I." So we ask again: Was sheol the inside of that fish? The answer is, figuratively yes, actually no. The words are *not* to be taken literally. Nor are our Lord's words to be taken literally, that he would be three days and three nights "in the heart of the earth."

It is the same with Ephesians 4:9, which says that our Lord "descended into the lower parts of the earth." I certainly believe that by "the lower parts of the earth" Paul meant hades (sheol), but I cannot think he meant underground. The phrase had become familiarly used of hades because the *body* was usually buried underground, and the grave had thereby become the symbol as well as the portal of what lay beyond.

Let me make a parallel. Six times in Matthew's Gospel our Lord warns men of gehenna, the final doom of the lost. As we all know, Gehenna was a deep ravine outside the wall of Jerusalem. Actually, the word is a slightly inexact transliteration of the Aramaic *Ge-hinnom,* a patronymic meaning "Valley of Hinnom." It was a real valley where the city refuse was dumped and burned, as also were carcasses of criminals and others. Is it surprising that it became a symbol of final punishment? Now when our Lord warned of gehenna, did he mean to be taken literally, as referring to that actual gorge outside the city? We all know better. He was using gehenna figuratively referring to a nonphysical reality. The same is true, so I believe, of that idiom, "the lower parts of the earth."

Or, referring again to Philippians 2:10—"That at the name of Jesus every knee should bow, of [beings] in heaven, and . . . in earth, and . . . under the earth . . ."—the compound Greek word translated as "under the earth" *(katachthon)* occurs nowhere else in the New Testament. In classical Greek, so far as I can find, it was never used of the solid earth's interior, but only figuratively of the infernal regions.

Again, that phrase "under the earth" reappears twice in the New Testament (though not the same Greek word) in Revelation 5:3 and 13. The second of those texts is noteworthy: "And every creature which is in heaven and on the earth and *under the earth* . . . I heard saying, To him who sits on the throne and to the lamb, Blessing and honor and glory and might, unto the ages of the ages." It pre-envisages a climax which must be still future, for not yet does every creature in heaven and on earth and "under the earth" exult in such a doxology. Nay, there is "war in heaven" between the dragon forces and those of archangel Michael; also millions on earth still rebel against saving truth; and there are millions in hades (sheol) who await judgment without any such song to God and the Lamb in their hearts. Surely that expression "under the earth" cannot mean an *underground* place where Satan and his insurrectionist consorts have their abode, or from where they carry on their anti-God warfare, for the archfiend and his host are definitively named "the prince of the power of the *air*" (Eph. 2:2) and the hosts of evil "in *the heavenlies*" (Eph. 6:12).

Nor, for further reasons, can I think that hades is some huge subterranean vault holding millions of disembodied human beings. When our Lord referred to the long-deceased Abraham, Isaac, and Jacob, and said, "God is not the God of the dead, but of the living" (Matt. 22:32), did he mean that those three patriarchs were living underground? To me, such an interpretation is weirdly unrealistic. What about Enoch who "walked with God, and he was not [or 'died not'] for God took him" (Gen. 5:24)? Did God take him underground? That, too, seems strangely incongruous. What about Moses, "whom Jehovah knew face to face" and whose body God himself "buried" (Deut. 34:6, 10)? Did God sink Moses' soul as well as his body underground? That, too, seems incompatible. What about Elijah, who "went *up*" in a chariot of fire "by a whirlwind into *heaven*" (2 Kings 2:11)? That certainly was "up," not down! Was it just a theatrical make-believe? Did God immediately afterward sink Elijah down to live beneath the soil of the earth? To me, that seems most indigestible.

Again, when Moses and Elijah suddenly appeared "in glory" with our Lord on the Mount of Transfiguration, did they give the slightest suggestion of having come from underground? Or, when they vanished, had they sunk back to some underground depth? Nay, their converse with our Lord about his coming "exodus" which he should "accomplish at Jerusalem" (Luke 9:31) suggests that they had come from a higher realm where they were well-informed about developments here on earth.

Are there *angels* in hades (sheol)? I should hardly think so. The thought of sinless angels always suggests the higher, the heavenly. What, then, of our Lord's words about poor beggar Lazarus, who, after his demise on earth, was "carried by the angels into Abraham's bosom" (Luke. 16:22)? Did they carry him to a "down-under" hades (sheol) beneath the earth's crust? That, to me, seems a strange anticlimax. Surely "Abraham's bosom" is somewhere *away* from earth, not *under* it. That is the clear impression given by our Lord's words. What, then, about the "rich man"? Our Lord says in the same verse that he "died and was buried, and in hades he lift up his eyes. . . ." So, is the hades to which the *ungodly* go deep under the ground? If so, how could that now disembodied man "under the earth" carry on that conversation (which our Lord reports) with Lazarus *away* from earth, in "Abraham's bosom?"

There are other passages which might be cited, such as Saul and the witch of Endor, which are similarly against the idea that sheol is under the ground, but maybe further references would be superfluous.

I well realize that perhaps these aspects prompt more questions than any of us can answer with certitude; but enough has been said, I think, to substantiate that sheol, the place of departed human spirits, is *not* somewhere beneath the earth's crust. Have we not also come across ample data to establish that sheol is not the same for the godly and the ungodly indiscriminately? There is a realm in sheol which looks upward into the light of God's face, even as there is a part which is a prison of gloom. The fact is, we are not meant to know where sheol (hades) is. It cannot be located as material abodes are; but the Old Testament witness to it is firmer and clearer than many have conceded.

MISAPPREHENDED TEXTS

The only other comment we need add concerns those who teach that sheol is a place of stark senselessness. They base their case on a few texts which, although cursorily seeming to favor that notion, are misunderstood.

One such is Ecclesiastes 9:10, "Whatsoever thy hand findeth to do, do it with thy might; for there is no work, nor device, nor knowledge, nor wisdom, in [sheol], whither thou goest." Do we need to point out again that those words express only a temporary opinion of Koheleth, and are not a "thus saith Jehovah"? In Ecclesiastes, as in Job, we must distinguish between what men thought and what God says. For instance, Job says, "He that goeth down to [sheol] shall come up no more" (Job 7:9); where as in 1 Samuel 2:6 *God* says, "The Lord . . . bringeth down to [sheol], and *bringeth up.*"

Much severer is David's dirge in Psalm 6:5, "For in death there is no remembrance of thee: in [sheol] who shall give thee thanks?" Viewed from an earthly standpoint, both members of that couplet are true. Death and departure to sheol *are* a great cutting off. The giving of thanks to God in the hearing of our fellows is ended. The lips are silenced. Nor is there even "remembrance" yonder in the way we remember God and his goodness here among our friends and neighbors. Praise and service such as David could render on earth, especially as anointed king of Israel, were not possible in the restricted life of sheol. To think of himself as *bodiless* made that other side of death seem shadowy and unsubstantial.

Elsewhere David makes brighter comments on sheol. Nonetheless, his thinking of it as a ghostly kind of existence is understandable. Even we Christian believers today, living in the larger light of the Christian revelation, find it easy to think that way. Our departed Christian loved ones are without bodies, without the physical senses, without face, figure, form. It is easy to think of them as vapoury, shadowy, aerified. Both inside and outside the Old Testament men in general thought of the departed as "shades" (Hebrew *rephaim:* Job 26:5; Prov. 2:18; Isa. 14:9; 26:19; see RSV and ASV margin). It is this present material world and this present life in the body which to people in general *seem* to be the solid reality, whereas the departed have disappeared into bodiless invisibility and depletion. Yes, that is how it looks from the earthward side: yet in fact that is the wrong way round. When our inner eyes are illumed we realize with the apostle Paul that "the things which are seen [here on earth] are temporal; but the things which are not seen [in the Beyond] are eternal" (2 Cor. 4:18). It is *here* that we are among the evanescent. It is *there* that we find the abiding realities.

Such, then, is the Old Testament teaching on sheol. All the way through we must distinguish between what men thought and what God himself says. What his Word actually says—and what it leaves *unsaid*—both guard us from the plentiful nonbiblical errors and fanciful speculations of those pre-Christian centuries. What the Old Testament *does* reveal is limited, but it prepares us for the fuller light shed upon it by the sunburst of further revelation through Christ.

NEW TESTAMENT TEACHINGS

For our present purpose, little further need be added to what we have already said about *hades,* but it is helpful to get the following facts clearly appreciated. Hades is the New Testament equivalent of the Old Testament sheol. Both words refer to the same sphere and state. The New Testament teaching confirms but also clarifies and amplifies that of the Old Testament.

First, there is the thrilling news that our Lord Jesus now holds the *"keys"* of sheol-hades. Hitherto, Satan held them. Hebrews 2:14 says that God the Son took to himself our human flesh and blood so that through death he might "destroy him that had *the power of death,* that is, the devil." In the permissive providence of God, Satan acquired that power when man disobeyed God and forfeited his own regality. Man sold himself to sin and death, and Satan claimed him. Human mortality and death came with their gloomy tyranny, and inasmuch as human sin virtually denied the divine ownership, Satan claimed all disembodied humans as his prisoners in sheol-hades. But now all that is changed. When our risen Savior appeared to John on the

Isle of Patmos his first announcement was, "I am the living One: I became dead, but behold I am alive to the ages of the ages, Amen; and *I have the keys of hades and of death!*" Thank God, the destinies of all human beings, both here and hereafter, are in those wondrous hands which once were nailed to the cross to save us!

UNDIMINISHED CONSCIOUSNESS

Second, that the departed now in sheol-hades are conscious and in possession of all their mental faculties is confirmed, emphasized, clarified. Between his crucifixion and resurrection our Savior-conqueror went into hades and "preached" to the millions there (1 Peter 3:18-20). That they were wide awake is further confirmed by 1 Peter 4:6, which adds that our Lord Jesus preached the Gospel to them. Reflect: millions of those disembodied humans had lived and died on earth without a glimmer of suspicion as to the nature of the one true God; and even those who had been brought up in Israel had died without the scantiest apprehension of God's great redemption plan. To all those unenlightened souls, our Lord made known the love of God now expressed through the atoning sacrifice on Calvary. He announced that eventually they should all be brought out of their sheol-hades confinement, and that there should be an absolutely righteous judgment with himself as the Judge, inasmuch as God had committed all judgment to his Redeemer-Son (John 5:22; Acts 17:31). His message was that although they had been hitherto darkly ignorant of God's nature and purpose, they should now think and live in hades "according to God" (1 Peter 4:6).

DIFFERENTIATION IN HADES

Third, the New Testament gives further enlightenment on the division between the godly and the ungodly in hades. I need not quote again the passage about the rich man and Lazarus in Luke 16, but we should lay to heart its solemn warning and description of that separation, with the "great gulf" between. It becomes the more arresting when we recognize that apparently our Lord was describing actual persons, not merely parabolic characters. There are those who insist that our Lord was using *only* a parable, and that the persons in it, even though representative, were fictitious. But if so, it is the only parable in which he *names* individuals, Lazarus and Abraham. My own persuasion is that he was delineating real persons and what they entered into on that other side of death. And how vividly it highlights all those other Scripture references to sheol-hades!

TRANSFORMING TRANSPLANTATION
Fourth, the New Testament clearly conveys that our Lord's resurrection and ascension have had a mighty repercussion in sheol-hades. The "paradise" or "Abraham's bosom" area of it has been (for want of a better word, perhaps) *transplanted* into what Paul calls "the third heaven" (2 Cor. 12:2). That hades-shaking surprise is signaled by Paul's elucidation in Ephesians 4:8-10, on which we commented earlier. Yes, think of it: "paradise" is now the "third heaven," and "Abraham's bosom" has become the bosom of our ascended Savior-King: and as a corollary of that comes the further disclosure that now, when Christian believers die, there is no going to hades, but an immediate transportation into the Savior's presence (2 Cor. 5:8).

ABOLITION OF HADES
Fifth, the Book of Revelation foretells the terminus and *abolition* of hades. The purpose which it now serves during the interval between death and resurrection will have been completed when the final judgment of the race takes place at the "Great White Throne." Revelation 20:11-15 describes that dread scene. We can imagine how awe-struck John was as, in supernatural vision, he watched the proceedings. He tells us what he saw. "And death and hades delivered up the dead which were in them: and they were judged every man, according to their works. And death and hades were

cast into the lake of fire. . . ." There is no more need for either the grave or for sheol-hades. Picture, if you can, those millions of souls disgorged from hades and arraigned before the great Judge of all. *Can* we picture it, or even faintly imagine it? A judgment of so vast a host, which would take hundreds of years if conducted by men here on earth, will be effected in an instantaneous, timeless concentration which is possible only to the infinite Creator and Judge of all. What a mind-prostrating scene indeed! But if you are a born-again Christian believer, lift up your heart with thanksgiving; for that Judge is your Savior! *You* will never be among the disgorged from sheol-hades, for you will never go there.

THE RESURRECTION BODY: WHEN?

Strange surprises sometimes come from unlikely quarters. Certain Bible scholars of note teach that Christian believers receive their resurrection body immediately after death. I quote from a learned Scottish professor: "The resurrection, that is to say, the assumption by the spirit [or soul] of its resurrection body takes place for the believer at death. . . . There is no interval between death and entrance on a glorified *embodied* existence." Often have I been indebted to the late Dr. W. N. Clarke's masterly *Outline of Christian Theology*. All the more, therefore, it disappointed me to find that he, too, held the same idea. "Each human being's resurrection," he says, "takes place at his death, and consists in the rising of the man from death to life in another realm of life. The spirit [or soul] does not rise thither alone, but receives whatever organism [body] is needed for its uses in that other life."

Yet although such respected names have been associated with that idea, I believe it to be demonstrably wrong, for the following reasons. (1) There is not one verse of Scripture which teaches it, nor can I find one which, when carefully considered, even implies it. (2) There are sufficient texts which clearly refute it, several of which we shall quote. (3) The idea seems to depend on an unworthy attitude to the inspiration of Scripture. For instance, the above-quoted professor has to admit that in 1 Thessalonians 4:13-18 and 1 Corinthians 15, Paul certainly does teach that all Christian believers will receive their resurrection bodies at the *second coming* of Christ, but he says that Paul's inspiration was faulty at that time; his thinking had not fully developed. Let me quote him, emphasizing certain words. "There seems to have been a development in Paul's thought which can be traced in his letters. In what is usually considered his earliest extant letter, 1 Thessalonians, written about A.D. 51, where he seems still to be under the influence of the pre-Christian Jewish eschatological conceptions in which, as a Pharisee, he had been brought up, Paul looks forward to a simultaneous general resurrection of the dead in Christ, and speaks of those in the graves being raised up at the 'Parousia' or 'Second Coming' of Christ. . . . But in his later writings, when he has let the specifically Christian revelation more and more determine his thought, we find that he has largely moved away from that point of view. . . . In 2 Corinthians 5:1-10 we find him suggesting that *at death* the believer becomes 'clothed upon' with the spiritual and immortal body which God gives."

It is a poor view of divine inspiration which has Paul thus "suggesting" later that what he had taught earlier was wrong. It is even worse to say that what he wrote in 1 Thessalonians and 1 Corinthians was "under the influence of pre-Christian Jewish eschatological conceptions" and not inerrantly inspired. What does Paul himself say about that? He says that the very words he used in his apostolic teachings were inspired by the Holy Spirit (1 Cor. 2:13). It is a clear-cut issue: either he was, or was not, supernaturally inspired in all he wrote. If what the professor calls Paul's "development" means that his later statements supplant or discount his earlier teachings, where are we?

What kind of inspiration is that? Real certainty is gone. Ever since the days of the German-originated rationalistic "higher criticism" that idea of a human "development" traceable in the Scripture writers has insinuated itself into theological thinking; and wherever it is received, it drains away faith in the true inspiration of the Bible.

However, even if, for the sake of argument, we were to grant some such "development" in Paul's thinking, it does not alter this fact, that both in his first epistle and in his last he taught that the resurrection of believers is *not until* the return of Christ. It is generally agreed that the latest of Paul's letters to the churches were Ephesians, Colossians, and Philippians. This is what he says in Philippians 3:20-21, "For our citizenship is in heaven, from whence also we look for the Savior, the Lord Jesus Christ, who shall [then] change this [present] body of humiliation, that it may be fashioned like unto his body of glory. . . ." So there we are: from first to last the teaching is that the bodily resurrection of believers is not until the return of our dear Lord.

Albeit, there is a final word to add. The above-quoted author says, "In 2 Corinthians 5:1-10 we find him [Paul] suggesting that at *death* the believer becomes 'clothed upon' with the spiritual and immortal body . . . so that there is no interval for the believer between death and the entrance upon full-embodied immortality." Yet the fact is that when 2 Corinthians 5:1-10 is read discerningly, it does *not* teach bodily resurrection at death. In the first five verses Paul certainly has his eye on that eventual resurrection body, the "house not made with hands, eternal in the heavens"; but in verse 6 he talks about our residence in this *present* body, which he calls, not a "house," but only a temporary "tabernacle." In *this* "tabernacle" he says, we "groan, being burdened" (v. 4) yet we are "always confident." Why? Because when death pulls down this tabernacle, the result is that to be "absent from the body" is to be—well, what? Is it to be "clothed upon with our immortal body"? No, not at all. Paul's word is that to be "absent from the body is to be *present with the Lord.*" There is simply no "suggestion" of a bodily resurrection *then*. On the contrary, Paul finalizes by adding, in verse 9, "Wherefore we labour, that, whether present [in this mortal body] or *absent* [from it], we may be accepted of him." So there *is* an interval of "absence from the body" between our demise on earth and the yet-future resurrection.

A STRANGE PECULIARITY

Going with this erroneous concept of a resurrection synchronizing with our bodily death is the peculiar supposition that because we Christians are already "risen with Christ" (Col. 3:1), and because his life-creating Spirit is in us, our present mortal bodies share in our spiritual development, until, by the time we pass into the world beyond, the body has reached a point where its transition from being a flesh-and-blood body into being a "spiritual body" is simply a completive sequence. Let me quote the professor again: "The resurrection experience has already begun to be realized by the believer in Christ. . . . Through the indwelling of the Spirit there is already going on a transfiguration of the whole personality, not merely of the soul, but of the bodily organ. . . . In the degree of development to which it [the body along with the soul] has attained at death, it will then be set free from the limitations of flesh and blood . . . to become a fitting organ [i.e., a non-flesh-and-blood body] in a more spiritual form of existence." With cordial respect I can only marvel that scholarly brethren can hold such a manifestly contradictory idea. It collides head-on with the real facts; for in a physical sense, old age, instead of being a "gradual transfiguration" is a gradual *deterioration* until, exhausted, the physical body closes its eyes in final expiry.

It seems strange, also, to think that the believer receives the resurrection body immediately after dying here, while the now-discarded physical body is lying in the grave. Scripture contains no such suggestion of *two* bodies belonging to the Christian.

There we must leave that peculiar aberration. It does not square with the full New Testament testimony. In one respect, however, one may feel a twinge of sympathy with it. If I am not mistaken, it is a revolt against another common mistake, namely, that when the Second Advent trumpet sounds and the "dead in Christ" are raised, they will receive the very same bodies as were laid in the grave or otherwise disposed of. That grossly material idea may have become widespread through the incautious wording in some of our well-known Christian creeds, but it is not scriptural. Hear Paul again: "Foolish man! What you sow does not come to life unless it dies. And what you sow is *not* the body which is to be, but a bare kernel, perhaps of wheat or of some other grain. . . . *So is it* with the resurrection of the dead. . . ." Those wonderful bodies which are yet to be ours will be the same in *structure* as these present mortal bodies, but they will be altogether different in *texture*. Instead of the perishable will be imperishability, the bloom and beauty of never-declining youth!

What a hope! Make haste, Lord Jesus. *Come quickly.* Thy saints in heaven and on earth are yearning for that day.

NINE

HEAVEN: WHERE AND WHAT?

In our English Bible (the King James Version) the words *heaven, heavens,* and *heavenly* occur 729 times (O.T. 434, N.T. 295). That overall figure breaks down as follows:

In the 434 *Old* Testament occurrences, 321 are in the singular, 113 plural. Always, when the word occurs in the plural, it means the *physical* heavens. As for the 321 which speak of "heaven" in the singular, about 235 mean the physical heaven, and about 86 the *abode of God,* the place where the throne of the Most High is.

Of the 295 *New* Testament occurrences, 219 are in the singular, and 20 plural; besides which there is the adjective *heavenly* 23 times, and the phrase "kingdom of heaven" (literally, "of the heavens") 33 times.

Note: Of the 219 times where the word *heaven* is in the singular, 71 times it means the *physical* heaven, though in some cases it could mean heaven either physical or spiritual or both. In the remaining 148 instances, it denotes heaven either as the abode and throne of God, where also the unfallen angels and other sinless intelligences are; or one or more of the supra-terrestrial regions where Satan and associated evil powers (but also holy intelligences) operate, and from where they affect mankind.

The adjective *heavenly* (23 times) means heaven in the divine sense (except in Ephesians, where the phrase "heavenly places" should be changed to "the heavenlies").

As for the title "kingdom of heaven" (literally, "kingdom of the heavens"), it means the kingdom which *comes* from heaven, in contrast to earthly kingdoms founded by men. It is the kingdom which "the God of heaven" will yet set up on earth at our Lord's return, which is why it is synonymously called "the kingdom of *God.*"

Perhaps nothing could be more fitting than to finalize this series by asking: What does the Bible teach about *heaven?* For most Christian believers, as also for many others brought up under Christian influence, heaven means one thing only, namely, the wonderful place where God centers his presence; where his throne is; where the flaming seraphim and the holy angels are; where the "many mansions" of the "Father's house" are; and where the "redeemed of the Lord" will live in sinless joys for ever. That concept of heaven, however, is too simplistic, too curtailed, as may be seen from the Scripture data given at the beginning of this present study. For our present purpose we need not go back again and travel through the Old Testament. The fuller biblical teaching came in with our Lord Jesus Christ and the New Testament writings. It is to those writings we now turn.

OTHER HEAVENS
The first thing to grasp is that besides the one heaven (singular) which most people think of, there are *other* heavens (plural) which we should carefully distinguish. Which are those *other* heavens? Where are they?

Even in the Old Testament a plurality of heavens is indicated, as in royal Solomon's noble laudation of Jehovah at the dedication of the temple: "The heaven of heavens cannot contain thee" (1 Kings 8:27). But such plural references are to the *physical* heavens rather than heavens in the sense of nonphysical regions inhabited by spirit-beings.

In the *New* Testament there is an eye-opening disclosure of nonphysical heavens surrounding our earth, or in close proximity to it, which are densely populated with higher and lower strata of supernatural intelligences. Let me call attention to some of the texts which reveal this.

THE "HEAVENLIES"
To begin with, there are those five passages in the epistle to the Ephesians where we have the expression "heavenly places." To be exact, in the Greek the phrase is "the heavenlies." Observe carefully what Paul says about them. First, in 1:3, he says,

> Who [God] hath blessed us with all spiritual blessings in *the heavenlies* in Christ.

Many Christians seem to think that Paul's phrase "the heavenlies" means no more than a high spiritual experience in the Christian life, but careful attention to the wording of Scripture soon shows that it means something decidedly different from that. Note Paul's second reference in chapter 1:20-22. He prays that we may know the working of God's mighty power,

> Which he wrought in Christ when he raised him from the dead, and set him at his own right hand in *the heavenlies,* far above all [every] principality and authority and lordship and every name that is named, not only in this age, but also in that which is to come; and hath put all things under his feet. . . .

Who can read those high-winging words without seeing that "the heavenlies" are a sphere occupied by spirit-intelligences classified into higher and lower ranks, where also our ascended Lord Jesus exercises control from a high stratum outranking all others? But turn now to the next reference, in chapter 2:5-6, which relates this to the Christian believer:

> Even when we were dead in sins [God] quickened us together with Christ (by grace ye are saved) and raised us up together, and seated us together in *the heavenlies* in Christ Jesus.

What does it mean to be "seated together" with our Lord in "the heavenlies"? Certainly we are not yet there locally in our resurrection immortality, but it at least indicates a union of our *minds* with him on his control-level up there, even while we are still living here on earth. A further aspect is added in the fourth of these Ephesian comments on "the heavenlies":

> Unto me, who am less than the least of all the saints, was this grace given, that I should preach among the nations the unsearchable riches of Christ, and to enlighten all as to what is the fellowship of the mystery which from the beginning of the ages has been hid in God who created all things by Jesus Christ, so that now, to the principalities and the authorities in *the heavenlies,* there might be made known through the church the manifold wisdom of God. (Eph. 3:8-10)

Such wording as that, of course, unmistakably lifts "the heavenlies" right away from being only a spiritual experience within the Christian. Clearly "the heavenlies" are a realm or area where nonhuman or superhuman beings exercise various functions and to whom God made known his many-sided wisdom when he disclosed his long-hidden secret, the *Ecclesia* or "Church." Those very numerous spirit-intelligences include both the unfallen angels and those who are now the sin-contaminated accomplices of Satan. Perhaps most striking of all is the fifth and final reference, in chapter 6:11-12:

> Put on the whole armour of God, that ye may be able to stand
> against the wiles of the devil. For we wrestle not against flesh
> and blood, but against principalities, against authorities, against
> the world-rulers of the darkness of this age, against the spirit-hosts
> of wickedness in *the heavenlies*.

That may well startle us. "The heavenlies" are the sphere
from which Satan masterminds his anti-God warfare and
invades our world of mankind by his waves of dark-minded
spirit-troops. That twelfth verse is an eye-opener. It tells
us that it is those evil insurgents from "the heavenlies"
who are the ruling force behind our sin-stricken world's
darkness!

Clearly, therefore, in those five Ephesian passages Paul's
phrase, "the heavenlies," cannot mean merely some high-
level experience within the believer. It denotes a populous
realm beyond mortal sight, inhabited by spirit-intelligences
both good and evil, both angelic and demonic. To grasp
that realistically is of mighty importance, for it has important bearings on the Christian life and on the meaning of
prayer.

CORRELATED OTHER PASSAGES

Look now into those other "heavens" a little more closely.
By comparing that phrase, "the heavenlies," with certain
other Scriptures we may learn further arresting signifi-
cances in it. For example, in Revelation 12:7-12 we read,

> There was war in heaven. Michael and his angels fought against
> the dragon, and the dragon fought and his angels and prevailed
> not, neither was their place found any more in heaven. . . . There-
> fore rejoice ye *heavens* and ye that *dwell in them*. Woe to the in-
> habitors of the earth and of the sea, for the devil is come down
> unto you, having great wrath because he knoweth that he hath
> but a short time.

Obviously the "heaven" where that "war" is waged cannot be the heaven where the Father's throne is and which

is the heavenly home of the redeemed, for in that heaven there is *no* war, no dragon-devil, no army of evil militants. So the "heaven" where archangel Michael routs the dragon-forces must be within the sphere to which Paul adverts in his phrase "the heavenlies." That indeed is confirmed by the words, "Therefore rejoice ye heavens [plural] and ye that dwell in them [plural]," the reason for the rejoicing being, of course, that at last those regions, (i.e., "the heavenlies") were being completely ridded of Satan and his allies.

So then, not only is there a plurality of heavens distinct from that "heaven of heavens" wherein is the throne of the Most High, but we begin to detect that "the heavenlies" uncovered to us in Ephesians are a realm of *close proximity to planet earth,* in fact seemingly everywhere around it. That ties in at once with Ephesians 2:2, where Satan is called "the prince of the power of *the air,*" or, bringing out the force of the Greek a little more floridly, "the arch-ruler of the *government* of the air."

Now of course the air, or atmosphere, is part of our *physical* world and its envelopment; yet although it can be felt and breathed it cannot be seen by human eyes any more than spirit-presences can. Revolting though it is, the invisible, close-clinging atmospheric surround of this earth is at present infested, utilized and contaminated by the equally invisible presence of Satan and his confederate hosts. Far worse than fog or smog, than fumes or chemical fallouts which vitiate the air and damage our bodies, is the unseen influence of Satan and his almost ubiquitously distributed demon-conspirators upon human *minds.* We may dismiss at once the notion of some early church fathers that storms and other atmospheric disturbances are due to Satan; but even the most cautious expositors are agreed that nothing less is meant than that the archfiend and his deployed emissaries *do* from the atmosphere infiltrate the thought-life of human beings, exerting strong pressures, urges, allurements, deceptions.

207

Quite apart from demon *possession* which, although on the increase today is comparatively fractional, there is widespread demon *persuasion* in the thinking of men and the affairs of nations. The blinder people are to that, the more it suits the arch-traitor's purpose. In considerable degree his spreading subordinates see us, watch us, know us. They cannot override human free will. Nor can they see directly into our minds, as God does. Nor are they everywhere. Nor can they influence all human beings individually all the time; for each of those evil predators, like all other created beings, is *finite* and therefore can be in only one place at any given instant. Nevertheless, they are legion in number and crafty in the pressures which they unsuspectedly exert on human minds, especially on those in administrative office.

Away back in Daniel 10:12-13, one of the angel princes belonging to that unseen realm, "the heavenlies," is sent in a visibly brilliant form to Daniel, and says,

> Fear not, Daniel, for from the first day that thou didst set thine heart to understand and to chasten thyself before thy God thy words were heard, and I am come for thy words. But the prince of the kingdom of Persia withstood me one and twenty days: but lo, Michael, one of the chief princes, came to help me; and I remained [or prevailed] there with the kings of Persia.

In that revealing disclosure we see *three* spirit-personalities from "the heavenlies," two of them holy, one of them evil. Two of them are titled "princes," indicating rank and command. One of the two holy princes (Michael) is designated a "chief prince" or "arch-prince," denoting a position of first command. The *evil* prince who hindered the holy prince's getting to Daniel is called "the prince of the kingdom of Persia," meaning that he had been delegated by Satan to corrupt as far as possible the ruling power there.

Later, in Daniel 10:20–11:1, the angelic prince who spoke to Daniel added, "And now I will return to fight with the prince of Persia; and when I go the prince of Greece [another of those spirit-warriors] will come. . . . There is none who supports me against these but Michael your prince [i.e., the archangel who specially stands up for the nation Israel: Dan. 12:1]. As for me, in the first year of Darius the Mede I stood up to confirm and strengthen him."

The implication is plain enough. Those angel personalities in "the heavenlies" are not only actively concerned in the affairs of men and nations on planet earth, but there are those of them, both the evil and the holy, who have specific campaign assignments in connection with governments and nations. Also, for our comfort, let us realize that just as Satan's angels are sent forth to work evil in our human race, so are *holy* angels sent forth to thwart and repulse them, and especially to safeguard Christian believers, who are the "heirs of salvation."

I believe we may reasonably infer that there are intelligences in "the heavenlies" who are particularly occupied with Soviet Russia, and others who are detailed to get the upper hand in the affairs of America. I believe that there are angels assigned to influence you and me, each of us; and how dear we are to those angels of Jesus! How tenderly they rejoice over even one human sinner who repents and comes to the Savior!

In 2 Corinthians 12:7 Paul tells us that "an angel of Satan" was deployed to "buffet" him continually—an ordeal which at that time had been going on for fourteen years. In Acts 27:23, Paul says to the captain and crew of a storm-battered ship in the Adriatic, "There stood by me this night an *angel of God* saying: Fear not, Paul; God hath given thee all them that sail with thee." We need not be surprised, therefore, that Paul's mind was often on "the heavenlies" from where such angels come.

Just how those spirit beings in "the heavenlies" make "war" who at present among earthly mortals shall say? At best we can only conjecture. They certainly do not use *physical* weapons, either the old-style metal or the modern nuclear. Must it not be somehow through collision of mind and will; of outgoing personal force either for the hindering or the furthering of good or evil on earth through human beings?

We might get a better glimpse into that if we knew just how Satan's angel harassed Paul, or how the Lord Jesus drove the legion of demons from the demoniac into the herd of swine, or how archangel Michael "contended" with the devil about the body of Moses (Jude 9). Particularly noteworthy is Gabriel's word to Daniel, that after arch-prince Michael had brought reinforcement, he (Gabriel) had "prevailed" with the rulers of Persia (ASV).

How Satan operates against the godly is seen in his un-detected oppression of Job. How he operates against the preaching of the Gospel is disclosed in 2 Corinthians 4:3, "If our Gospel is veiled it is veiled in them that are perishing, in whom the god of this age hath blinded the minds of the unbelieving" (ASV). All of us who are Christian workers need to recognize that behind every activity of evil on earth today, behind all anti-Godism and perversion of truth, is the ugly scheming of the supreme liar, Satan.

HINTS FROM PARAPSYCHOLOGY?

Today, perhaps without our suspecting it, strange clues pertaining to that spiritual warfare in "the heavenlies" may be coming to us from the startling discoveries being made by parapsychologists. Hitherto, most people have regarded telepathy, clairvoyance, extra-sensory perception, tele-kinesis, and other such psychic peculiarities as being no more than strange mental quirks, sly guesswork, trickery, or uncanny premonition; but they are soon to be shaken out of such superficial ideas. Extraordinary developments are on the way today through serious scientific investiga-tion. In fact, what is known as "parapsychology" is now assuming a frightening potentiality as the ultimate military weapon.

As we all know, there have been, and are, "psychic" persons able to *will* certain objects into motion. Until now, on hearing of such seeming irrationalities, all we could say was, "How strange!" or "How funny!" (e.g., the stopping of a frog's heart solely by concentratedly willing it; the diagnosing of puzzling diseases simply by mental focus; the detection of crime and criminals without external clues; the moving of solid objects [psychokinesis] by the power of mind over matter; the uncanny foretelling of coming events).

Now, however, all these and other psychic singularities are the subject of intense scientific research, with quite staggering results. Soviet Russia is spending millions of dollars a year on such parapsychological investigation by top-rank scientists—hundreds of them. Psychics are rounded up, their strange abilities cultivated and monitored, their minds and brains intensively studied, to find out how the laws of cause and effect operate in extrasensory perception and other related mental abnormalities. Progress has been stunning. Human skulls have been split open solely by psychic power at a mile distant. Living subjects miles away have been forced to obey telepathically transmitted commands!

Dr. Jeff Eerkens, nuclear engineer and specialist on Russian psychics, says, "We believe the Russians have discovered that an energy field constantly flows around the earth at the speed of light, and that the human brain, acting just like a radio transmitter, can put electrically charged thoughts into this stream of energy which carries it along until another brain, acting like a radio receiver, picks it up."

But much more: All the increasing parapsychological "know how" is being linked with apparatus such as "psychotronic generators" which store psychic energy. And in Russia all this hitherto unrealized potential inside the human mind is being harnessed to Soviet military technique. Dr. Eerkens further says, "It means that the Soviets could tune in to anyone's thoughts, including Western military leaders. . . . Using another application of the same new scientific principles they could drive a man mad.

Theoretically, they could brainwash him, induce heart attacks or strokes from thousands of miles away. The signals could command the brain to stop functioning, or the heart to stop beating. We know they have done this with small animals; . . . there doesn't seem to be much difference in applying it to human beings."

Those quotations are taken from a powerful pamphlet, *The Mind Control Plot,* by Dr. W. S. McBirnie, a scholarly analyst of world affairs, who also quotes the noted Israeli psychic, Uri Geller: "In maybe ten or fifteen years Soviet psychics will be able to sabotage every military warning system and every weapon system in the West. We know the Russians are training psychics like Kulagina totally to erase commands and information stored on computer tapes which control today's sophisticated weapons." Devices are being perfected to work Soviet will on human minds here in the West; and advanced experiments are under way aimed at "spying psychically, using long-range telepathy on Western leaders."

Much more might be added, but sufficient evidence is furnished by the foregoing cullings to suggest that the ultimate in human warfare will not be nuclear weapons but the power of *mind.* Could it be, then, that we are getting clues as to how war is waged by spirit-powers in that realm which Paul calls "the heavenlies"?

HIGHER AND LOWER HEAVENS

Furthermore, there are heavens higher than those so far mentioned. We infer that they are not as near to our globe. Hebrews 4:14 says, "We have a great High Priest who has passed *through* the heavens" (plural). Hebrews 9:24 adds, that having passed beyond those, He "entered into heaven *itself* [singular] now to appear in the *presence of God.* " Ephesians 4:10 has the parallel comment that our Lord ascended up "far above *all* the heavens." So there are higher and lower heavens, and there is that supreme heaven which distinguishingly is "heaven itself"—called in Hebrews 8:1 "the throne of the Majesty in the *heavens.*"

We can scarcely think of those higher and lower heavens as being in geographical layers, for there is no physical geography in a purely spiritual existence. Yet it does seem as though "the heavenlies" to which Paul refers in Ephesians must be the lowest of them in this sense; that they are sublunary, infested by Satan and his evil forces, the nearest to this earth, and more or less coextensive with the vapory expanse around it. Also, with the data before us which we have just gathered we see that in *all* the heavens our resurrected, ascended, glorified, wonderful Lord Jesus is omnipotently *supreme.*

Which heaven, then, is it into which our departed Christian loved ones have gone, and to which we ourselves are going, if we are saved through the precious blood of Jesus? That question involves some huge considerations, some of them astronomical. The magnitude of the starry heavens and the seeming infinitudes of space utterly baffle human comprehension. Gone forever are the days when our comparatively infinitessimal earth was thought to be the center of the universe. That this speck of solidified gas could ever be thought of as a cosmic center is now astronomically comical. Gone forever, also, are the days when our solar system was regarded as the central wonder in creation. Our sun, with all its nine planets and asteroids swinging round it is but a dwarf in the particular system to which it belongs, while in relation to the whole universe it is about as large, comparatively, as a grain of sand in the Sahara desert.

Light, like electricity, travels at a velocity of some 186,330 miles per second. As every schoolboy nowadays knows, so immense are the reaches of the universe that they have to be measured in "light years." Even then they are quite beyond human imagination. As larger telescopes were made, the number of stars discernible soon became over 80 million, but the number photographed after the installing of the 100-inch Mount Wilson reflector was 1.5 billion. Still later, when the Palomar telescope began operating in 1949, theoretically capable of penetrating 2 billion light years into space, 30 billion stars could be photographed. It is estimated that with some further super-telescope, billions more would crowd into view, each one (or largely so) like the millions already discovered, with its own solar system. Human imagination is stunned.

I remember gasping, years ago, as I read that by sound-wave photography, stars had been photographed "20 million light years away," and that "20 million light years *away*" meant, really, "20 million light years *ago*," because it had taken 20 million light years for the rays from those stars to reach our telescopes. The strange-seeming, awesome fact is that we do not see those stars as they now are. Of their present existence or expired existence we have no knowledge. We see them only as they were, ten, twenty, or a hundred thousand years ago, or more. They may have passed into nothingness ages ago in terms of earthly reckoning. We cannot know until the rays of light from them reach us with the information—rays which may be on their lightning-swift but long, long flight to tell us of some conflagration aeons ago, or that a whole system of worlds was then destroyed.

The "light year" as a standard by which to measure astro-spatial distances and dimensions has been called "the celestial yardstick." In one year light travels about 6 trillion miles (6,000,000,000,000). By that method of reckoning, Sirius, one of the brightest stars in our skies, is 8 light years distant from earth. Vega, the bright blue star in the constellation of Lyra, is 26 light years away. Arcturus, the giant fixed star in the constellation of Bootes, is 41 light years out yonder. The stars of the Plough, or Great Bear, are 80 light years from us, and Betelgeuse, the red star of Orion, 190 light years away. The stars of the Pleiades above Orion are 350 light years away, and Rigel, the blue star 540 distant. The cluster of stars in the constellation of Hercules is no less than 36,000 light years away! Those bewildering measurements can be worked out in miles, approximately, if we multiply the above figures by 186,330 x 60 x 60 x 24 x 365¼ (60 for seconds per minute, 60 for minutes per hour, 24 for hours per day, 365¼ days per year).

It astonished the world some years ago when Dr. E. P. Hubble of Mount Wilson Observatory calculated the boundaries of the "metagalaxy" (the "universe" next to our own) as not less than 6,000 light years in diameter, and containing 500 million galaxies. Since then the Palomar telescope, with its far more powerful reach, has swept the skies, only to reveal that the bigger the telescope the vaster the heavens grow. Even *Proxima Centauri,* the nearest star to our little globe, is 25 trillion miles away, and light from it takes over four years to cross the gulf of space between it and us.

WHERE, THEN, IS HEAVEN?

All these recent revelations of the celestial spheres and their magnitude poignantly point up the question: *Where,* then, are the millions of departed Christians? Have they been swept "light years" away from earth to some "heaven" millions upon millions of miles distant, somewhere amid those Gargantuan constellations and voluminous outer spaces? I think the answer to that question has to be no, for certain cogent reasons.

Space has dimensions. It can be measured. It has directions: forward, backward, sideways, upward, downward. It has nearness and farness. To move in it from one point to another involves a going and a coming. When the Bible speaks of angels visiting this earth it indicates a coming *from* somewhere in the heavens *to* some place here on earth. Such movement from and to incurs succession: in other words, it takes *time.* Just as light, in speeding through space, takes measurable time, so do personal beings, whether with or without physical bodies.

All created personal beings are finite and therefore local,

whether seraph, archangel, angel, Satan, demon, human being. All are finite and, from moment to moment, *local:* they can be in only one place at any given instant. If they move from one point to another there is motion, succession, *time.* So, if our departed Christian loved ones are "light years" (millions and millions of miles) away, they must have taken corresponding time to reach there; and it would take equal time for them to return to earth. What, then, of the Scripture teaching that at our Lord's return to this earth the multi-thousands of departed saints will accompany him, to receive their resurrection bodies and to share in his millenial earth-rule?

If our Lord's return is now near, as the signs certainly seem to indicate, then those departed tens of thousands simply cannot get back in time to join him; nor could they get here even for the end of the Millennium and the dissolution of the Adamic regime and the bringing in of the new heaven and earth—not if they are many light years away. One cannot speak with anything like dogmatism on such a matter, for it cannot be entirely free from conjecture; yet I believe that what I say is at least realistic. My own pondered conviction is that the Christian departed have gone to a "heaven" somewhere near planet earth, and that they have a far more intimate cognizance of earthly goings on than we have hitherto suspected.

OUR NEAREST PLANETARY NEIGHBOR

Some time ago I found a group of Christians (professedly representing many others) selling the idea that the heaven to which Christians go is the planet Venus. To me, their enthusiasm was far greater than their reasoning. Admittedly, as seen from our earth, Venus is the brightest of the planets by reason of its being the closest to us of all the heavenly bodies, and because its disc often has a dazzling brilliance due to the high reflection of sunlight by the cloud mass continually enveloping it. At times, indeed, it is so bright in our sky that people write to their newspaper editors asking, "What was that brilliant 'star' in the sky last night?"

Yet who on earth would want to live there? Although a beautiful object to the telescope, it is most inhospitable as a habitat. It has an oppressive atmosphere and a surface pressure ninety times that of earth. At its lower altitudes its air is strongly sulphurous. Oxygen is very rare. Its very hot temperature and sky-darkening cloud-blanket and noxious environment are "extremely hostile to life as we know it."

Yes, who would wish to live *there*, "whether in the body or out of the body" (2 Cor. 12:3)? Far better stay on earth! In any case, why should departed Christians pass as disembodied *spirits* to another *physical* abode? Most definitely they do not need any such planetary rendezvous between death of the body and the coming resurrection. And after we have all received our resurrection bodies we certainly will not need Venus to give us heavenly joy. No, that neighbor planet may then be a nearby resort for postmillenial picnics now and then, but it can never compete with Planet Earth when the New Jerusalem is here! The novel Venus theory of heaven is wrong. There is not a scintilla of evidence or suggestion to support it in Scripture. It may be dismissed as illusory.

THE EMPTY SPACE IN THE NORTH

There is a rather engaging theory that heaven is in the "empty space of the north," that is, the apparently "empty space" in the celestial region north of our earth. Let me quote from a booklet advocating that.

> About thirty years ago it was discovered that there are no stars in the heaven due north of our planet. . . . For years astronomers have been photographing the heavens, and now they have found that due north . . . there is an empty space. What is that empty space? It is the parted way to heaven. When you pass out of this world you will not have to find your way, for there is a clear passage up to heaven.

The theory seems unaware of the *several* heavens which Scripture distinguishes. By "heaven" the theory means solely the heaven which is concentratedly the dwelling place of God; the heaven of sinless rapture which is the eternal home of the redeemed. The teaching also assumes that Christian believers go there immediately on departing from earth.

Some of the Scripture passages which seem to lend themselves to that idea are intriguing. One is Job 26:7: "He [God] stretches out the *north* over empty space, and hangs the earth on nothing" (ASV). Those two statements taken together seem to indicate that the "north" spoken of is not merely somewhere north on the earth, but somewhere in an "empty space" beyond it.

In Isaiah 14:13-14, Lucifer is represented as saying, "I will ascend into heaven, I will exalt my throne above the stars of God; I will sit also upon the mount of assembly in the uttermost parts of the *north* . . . above the heights of the clouds . . . like the Most High." That passage, also, seems to imply that "the north" there spoken of is beyond the earth, somewhere in the celestial sphere.

Again, in the first chapter of Ezekiel, where the prophet describes his prostrating vision of the heavenly cherubim, those wondrous beings who apparently live closest of all creatures to the throne of the Deity, we are told how the vision unfolded until, climactically, Ezekiel saw a "likeness" of the One who sits on that awesome throne. Just as clearly as Isaiah's transforming vision (Isaiah 6) was a vision of the divine throne in heaven, so was Ezekiel's; and it is notable that it swept over him on a "whirlwind out of the *north*"—as though the north was the *abode* of those flashing cherubs and of that sapphire throne.

There are yet other references to the north which, although only incidental, may possibly be corroborative. Leviticus 1:11 instructs that the burnt offering must be slain "on the side of the altar *northward* before the Lord," as though northward looked toward Jehovah. Albeit, whether there *was* such a significance in that instruction seems doubtful to my own mind. It is not given with the other sacrifices. May not the north side have been only a matter of convenience? West of the altar was the "holy place." East of it was the place for the heap of ashes (Lev. 1:16). South, as Josephus seems to indicate, was the "ascent to the altar." So, was it not for *those* reasons that the north was chosen for the slaying?

Another text said to tie in with the locating of heaven in the "empty space" of the north is Psalm 75:6-7: "For promotion cometh neither from the east, nor from the west, nor from the south. But God is the judge: he putteth down one, and setteth up another." The argument is, that since promotion does not come from the other three points of the compass it must come from the *north*, from "God the judge." That inference, however, is weakened inasmuch as the Hebrew word translated "south" in our King James Version means, strictly, desert or wilderness, and is so rendered in all recent translations.

Even so, the "empty space" theory might still hold were it not that the *stars* contradict it—which raises an interesting point pertaining to our earth's orbiting round what is called "the celestial equator." It can be explained fairly simply. Here in America, when an airplane rises from the ground, we say it is going "up," which would seem to imply that when an airplane does likewise in Australia on the under and opposite side of our globe it goes in the opposite direction, (i.e., down). Yet the people in Australia just as naturally say it is going "up" as we do in America. The fact is, of course, that whether there or here, the plane goes "off" rather than "up." Is there, then, any place on earth from which one can really go "up?"—not just "up north" *on* the earth, but up north *from* the earth into space? The booklet to which I have referred says, yes, it is the north pole. Let me quote.

The world rotates continuously on its axis, but there is one point that never changes: that is, due north. When you look north you are looking *up*. North is always top of the map.

It is to the north that the needle of the compass always points. That is where the north *star* shines, often called the "pole star." Heaven, therefore (says the booklet) is "up" because it is *north*, and it is somewhere in the "empty space" up there.

Yet that is just where the theory cracks, or so it seems to me. When Job spoke of the "north" and of the "empty space," some 3,600 years ago or more, was the pole star *then* the same as the pole star *now?* Was the stellar "north," as seen from the earth, the same then as now? Was the "empty space" to which Job referred *then* the sidereal gap which is said to be seen north of our planet *now?* I think the answer is no.

Take another look at planet earth and its space-journeying. Besides rotating on its axis and revolving round the sun, it reels like a huge gyroscope round an imaginary line perpendicular to the plane of the earth's equator, but it does so with such slow motion that it takes nearly 2,900 years to make one complete revolution of its axis around it. Further, as the earth travels slowly in its circuit round that perpendicular line its axis points successively to different parts of the heavens. The point in the heavens to which earth's axis points is called the celestial pole. And because the earth's axis points directly to it, that celestial pole will seem fixed while all the stars will appear to revolve round it, or round the *star* which is nearest to it, and which at that time will be called the pole star.

In line with that, 4,000 years ago, or a bit later when Job spoke about the "empty space" in the "north," the earth's axis pointed in a different direction from that in which it points today. The constellations *then* would appear in a different part of the skies from that in which we see them today. The earth's axis or pole was then pointing to

Thuban, the brightest star in the constellation of Draco. That was the pole star *then.* It was the pole star, also, to the Egyptians when they built the great pyramid of Cheops. But it is *not* the pole star today in relation to the earth. Our pole star, or "north star," today is Polaris, the alpha star of Ursa Minor.

So earth's "north" and "up" into space today are *not* what they were to patriarch Job. Any "empty space" which may be discerned in the sidereal heavens today cannot be that to which Job's words apparently alluded long ago. Therefore, if *heaven* was due "north" in Job's time it just cannot be, with any exactness, up from the earth due north today. It seems to me, therefore, that the testimony of the stars is against the "empty space in the north" theory.

Even more decisive against it is that it wings departed Christians away beyond earth and loses them amid those seemingly interminable "light year" distances—an idea which, to my own mind, is incredible. In fact, the booklet already quoted falls into a self-contradiction in that connection. On one page its author says that the Scriptures distinguish three heavens: (1) the lower heaven of the clouds; (2) the planetary and stellar heavens; and (3) the heaven of heavens, the abode of God. And on another page he says, "Above and beyond the stars there is the third or highest heaven. Into that heaven every true believer will pass at death." Yet if "heaven" is *beyond* the stars, how can it be, as the booklet elsewhere claims, in the "empty space" north of this earth, whole light years nearer to us? All considered, we must reject the "empty space" theory as both exegetically and astronomically untenable.

SCRIPTURAL INDICATIONS
So far our enquiry has shown us where heaven is not, rather than where it is. It leaves us asking: Are there reliable clues? I think there are. Let this be clear, however, that by "heaven" I now mean not the "heaven of heavens," the supposedly one-and-only heaven meant in the above-quoted booklet,

the heaven which is the eternal divine ultimate. No, I mean the "heaven" to which Christians go upon vacating the mortal body and passing from earth. As for that heaven, I believe there are some fairly clear scriptural pointers. My persuasion is that it is somewhere near this earth. Scriptural indications and sanctified common sense alike, so it seems to me, lead us to that belief.

That oft-quoted text, 2 Corinthians 5:8, says of Christian believers that to be "absent from the body" is to be "present with the Lord." *Where* is our Lord? If there is a clear answer to that, we may be well on our way to knowing where the heaven is to which our Christian kin have gone.

There again, however, as soon as we ask where our ascended Savior now is, we are face to face with a profound mystery, namely, his conjoined humanity and deity. The Christ of the New Testament is no mere demigod of the Jehovah's Witnesses type, nor one whose humanhood was illusory, after the Christian Science notion. The real Christ of Scripture is both truly God and truly Man. He is not only "the Son of God," he is *God the Son,* coequal with the eternal Father in all the divine attributes and plenitudes. In that sense he is in *every* place and confined to none. He is on the throne of the Deity in the "heaven of heavens" yet at the same time exquisitely near you and me this minute here on renegade planet earth.

What we are particularly wanting to know is: Where is he now *bodily?* His divine presence fills everywhere, but his body is *local.* He rose from the grave bodily. He ascended to heaven bodily. He is somewhere now bodily, and therefore *locally.* Where is he now in that resplendent resurrection body?

Various verses tell us that he is now in "heaven." Others add that he is at the "*right hand* of God" (Mark. 16:19; Rom. 8:34; Eph. 1:20; Heb. 10:12; et al.). Others place him in "the *throne* of God" (Heb. 8:1; Rev. 3:21; 5:6; et al.). So where is God's "right hand"? Where is his "throne"? Need it be said that the expression, God's "right hand" is anthropomorphic? God is a Spirit. Therefore he does not have either hands or other bodily organs. Equally, when Scripture speaks of his throne it does so merely metonymically; for God, being purely spiritual, does not have a physical throne. By God's right hand and throne, Scripture means his active omnipotence and government. And where that is, there *Jesus* is, in his radiant body.

That brings us a step nearer to the answer we are seeking. When the British Empire was at its greatest, and Queen Victoria was reigning over it, where was her throne? It was in London, England. But was it only there? No. In a secondary but quite real sense her throne was in India, Australia, Canada, and other parts of the empire through its officers of the Crown. So is it with the throne of God; but there is one place just now where it is *specially* operative because of the Satan-and-sin tragedy connected with our Adamic race. That place is a "heaven" *near* our earth; and there are several texts which, taken together, converge to indicate so.

One is Hebrews 4:14 (ASV), which says that as our "great high priest," the Lord Jesus, "passed *through* the heavens" (plural). Another is Ephesians 4:10, which says that he "ascended up far above *all* heavens." Another is 2 Corinthians 12:2. It speaks of the "third heaven" which immediately afterward is called "paradise" (v. 4)—and we know from Luke 23:43 that Jesus is *there*. We have seen how incorrect it is to think of those three heavens as the heaven of the clouds and the heaven of the stars and a supposed "heaven of heavens" *beyond* the stars. Also, as already noted, it is misleading to think of them as higher and lower in the sense of geographical layers; for those three heavens are spiritual, not material.

The mists are clearing! Besides "heaven" (singular) there are "heavens" (plural). Of such heavens there seem to be three. The third, and highest in the sense of authority, power, holy society, felicity, and in its glory of the divine presence there, is also called "paradise" because of its sinless rapture: and *that* is where our risen Lord is *bodily*. In one sublime aspect he is *above* even that "third heaven." As Hebrews 7:26 and Ephesians 4:10 tell us, he is "higher than the heavens" and "far above all heavens." He is so in the sheer glory of his divine-human *person*. Yet nonetheless he is accentuatedly present in that "third heaven," paradise, in a supremely beatific way—not only personally, but *bodily* and *visibly,* the seen and adored King of kings among his redeemed and translated people.

Perhaps the most arresting texts confirming all this are those five in Ephesians where Paul uses that phrase, "the heavenlies." In chapter 1:20-21, he prays that we might know inwardly the power of God "which he wrought in Christ when he raised him from the dead and set him at his own right hand in *the heavenlies,* far above every principality and authority and power and lordship. . . ." That phrase, "the heavenlies," has become more significant to us now. Quite strikingly it includes all the three heavens. In the text just quoted we see our Lord Jesus there, high over all, in that "third heaven." Next, in chapter 2:6, Christian believers are viewed as sitting "together" there, "in Christ Jesus." Then, in chapter 3:10, we see all "the principalities and the authorities"—all intelligences, both the holy and the unholy, apparently in the intermediate heaven. Finally, in Ephesians 6:12, we see the evil hosts of Satan operating, as it would seem, in the lowest area: "We wrestle not against flesh and blood, but against principalities, against authorities, against the world-rulers of the darkness of this age, against the spirit-powers of wickedness in *the heavenlies.*"

Curiosity sometimes gets the better of me, and I find myself wanting to see those realms comprising "the heavenlies"; but most of all I begin now to enter into Paul's "desire to depart and to be with Christ" on that highest level, the "third heaven." Yes, that is the paradise where our glorious Lord Jesus now reigns in bodily, visible regality. That is where the heavenly "mansions" are. That is where he "prepared a place" for all the saints who are now with him there, and where he is preparing a place for you and me, if we are truly his. Should it be that we join the heavenly host there before our Lord returns to this earth, that is the "heaven" from which we shall accompany him in the overwhelming splendor of his descent. What a paradise indeed that third heaven must be! No wonder that Paul, having been "caught up" and allowed to peer into it, had a "desire to depart" from earth and to be there!

WHAT IS THE KIND OF LIFE THERE?

But finally, *what* is that heaven? What is its nature? What is it experientially? Many will reply: Who on earth can answer such a question? How can we have even the faintest advance concept of it while we are confined in these earthen bodies with their limiting physical senses?

That reaction I duly appreciate. Shortly before my godly mother went to heaven she said to me, "Sid, I have read everything the Bible says about heaven. It all adds up to something very wonderful, but, even so, our physical senses give us no reliable clue as to what living in that purely spiritual realm will be. We cannot know until we are there."

True! Yet the human mind can grasp, to some degree, realities which are above physical and temporal boundaries, for the mind is itself spiritual and supersensuous, even though at present operating restrictedly through a sensory organism. In Ephesians 1:17-18, Paul prays that God "may give unto you the Spirit of wisdom [insight] and revelation [unveiling] the *eyes* or your *mind* being *illumined,* that you may know [lit. inwardly *see*] . . ." Think of it: "insight," "unveiling," "eyes," "mind," "illumined," "see"! What a ministry of the Holy Spirit to us! And it is real. To those sanctified and prayerful Christian believers who in inward experience "sit together" with Christ in "the heavenlies"

(Eph. 2:6), it is so real that at times they feel as though they are virtually there!

I speak with due carefulness and reverence when I add that outstanding men and women of God have left testimony to the way they have been lifted there in times of rapt communion with our Lord, and have inwardly "seen," known, *felt* something of the pure bliss enveloping that heavenly summerland. With adoring gratitude even some of ourselves can bear witness to experiences akin to those. To all of us the Holy Spirit can make spiritual realities "come alive"—by which I mean no mere excitement of imagination, but his ministry of inward *revelation*. My thoughts go back again, now, to Revelation 7:9-17 with its apocalyptic portrayal of the raptured saints amid the glory of that upper heaven.

> After this I beheld, and, lo, a great multitude which no man could number, of all nations and kindreds and people and tongues, stood before the throne and before the Lamb, clothed with white robes, and with palm branches in their hands.
>
> And they cried with a loud voice, saying, Salvation to our God who sitteth upon the throne, and unto the Lamb.
>
> And all the angels stood round about the throne and the elders and the four living beings, and fell before the throne on their faces, and worshipped God, saying, Amen: Blessing and glory and wisdom and thanksgiving and honour and power and might be unto our God for ever and ever. Amen.
>
> And one of the elders answered, saying to me: What are these which are arrayed in white robes? and whence came they? And I said unto him, Sir, thou knowest. And he said to me, These are they which came [lit. are *coming,* i.e., some already there and others continually joining them] out of great tribulation, and have washed their robes and made them white in the blood of the Lamb.
>
> Therefore are they before the throne of God, and serve him day and night in his temple: and he that sitteth on the throne shall dwell among them. They shall hunger no more, neither thirst any more, neither shall the sun strike on them, nor any burning heat. For the Lamb which is in the midst of the throne shall feed them, and lead them unto living fountains of waters; and God shall wipe away all tears from their eyes.

We do not forget, of course, that it is all symbol; spirits do not wear actual garments. But the symbols represent realities. The value of having it in symbol, rather than in ordinary statement, is that symbol makes it vivid photographically to our minds. Think, then, of the portrayal which the above passage gives us of those saints in that surpassing glory.

First, there is the realization of *final release*. Not a wisp of a hint that they have been intermediately quarantined in some purgatory or soul-sleep of human invention! Unmistakably, they have come there by immediate translation from earthly tribulation to that heavenly compensation. All of them have come out of "great tribulation." They have been coming there ever since the Gospel was first preached, and the church was founded, and the great red dragon started persecuting the followers of the Lamb; not only out of "tribulation" in the sense of persecution, but, as the Greek word suggests, out of all hurtful pressure, trouble, affliction, temptation. Many have come from jails, concentration camps, sickbeds, poverty, loneliness, hunger and thirst. But all that is now over forever. The deliverance is absolute. They know it. They feel it. They thrill to it, and break into spontaneous song before the heavenly throne.

Second, they experience *utter holiness*. That is what those white robes attest. How did they come by that spotless whiteness? They "washed their robes in the blood of the Lamb." So those white robes do not represent the substitutionary righteousness of *Christ* which is imputed to all believers, making them *legally* righteous; for *that* righteousness can never be either defiled or "washed." No, those white garments signify blemishlessness of moral *condition*. Not a trace or lingering scar of sin! In the words of Jude 24, they are presented "*faultless* before the presence of his glory with exceeding joy." They have become transformed into the image of their holy Redeemer. "His name shall be in their foreheads." They radiantly reflect "the King

227

in his beauty" (Rev. 22:4; Isa. 33:17).

Third, they enjoy *open vision of God*. In Jehovah's tabernacle on earth the Shekinah was curtained off from human eyes, but in the heavenly paradise it shines forth directly from him that sitteth on the throne, interpenetrating all the denizens there. As the Scripture says, "they are before the throne of God," and "He that sitteth on the throne shall dwell among them." They are enrapt by that glory-light "which no man on earth can approach unto." That blaze of the divine holiness which would be torture unbearable to the unclean is pure bliss to the elect in heaven. Besides which, they now see their beloved Shepherd face to face; not as he was in Nazareth or Capernaum or disfigured on Calvary, but as he now is in the gentle splendor and immaculate loveliness of his exaltation—which joy even apart from all else is very heaven to them.

Next, they exult in *everlasting victory*. The white robes and waving palm branches proclaim it. How often white signifies victory! It is on a "white cloud" that Jesus comes to crush the Anti-Christ at Armageddon. On "white horses" the armies of heaven follow him. It is on a "Great White Throne" that he at last judges our human race. White is the opposite of black, the color of defeat and death, even as the palm is the symbolic opposite of the weeping willow. Those waving palm leaves in the hands of yonder white-robed throng betoken victory celebration, and well they might, for Satan, the false angel, the ravening lion, the cunning fowler, the poisonous reptile, the "deceiver," the "adversary," the lying Beelzebub, and his evil legions, are finally beaten by the Lord's overcomers. The apostle John is among them, singing, "This is the victory that overcometh the world, even our faith." Paul is there, exclaiming, "We are more than conquerors through him that loved us." Many of them, when they were on earth "loved not their lives unto death" and all of them "overcame by the blood of the Lamb"; and now they "reign with Christ" in victory unto "the ages of the ages."

Again, they are engaged in *active ministry*. Those white robes are a vesture indicating royal priesthood, even as clean white linen was the main fabric in the garb of Israel's Aaronic priesthood long ago. In that upper heaven, those "spirits of just men made perfect" apparently need no instruction classes as a preliminary to their commencement on celestial employ. Not only do they at once engage in vocal adoration, ascribing "salvation to our God which sitteth upon the throne" but they also "serve him day and night in his temple" (Rev. 7:15). True enough, it is but symbol, but it depicts what is actual. No angels are needed to instruct those "saints in light" as to the customs of that heavenly realm, for even while they were on earth their "citizenship was in heaven" and their life was "hid with Christ in God." They take naturally to their new environment in Immanuel's land. They need no initiation into its sacred mysteries, for through many lingerings in prayer while on earth they "entered into the veil" and learned "the secret of the Lord." The white robes display their immediate fitness as believer-priests for service on that higher level.

Their heaven is no place of idle contemplation, but consists of soul-satisfying activities; for up yonder there are "diversities of operations" and the Holy Spirit is continually "dividing to every man severally as he wills." There is never any tiredness in service, for they continually drink of "living waters" which "renew their strength" and give them immortal animation.

Once again, their condition is one of *ecstatic joy*. Here on earth, too much ecstacy would be insupportable to these fragile nervous systems of ours, but up there the ineffable rapture is altogether supersensory, and the mental state of those who experience it is so superior to anything known on earth that words cannot describe it. They are immortal. Their capacities are supernatural. Their minds and motivation are sinless. Their experience of God is sublime. Their energy is boundless. They "mount up with wings as eagles." They "run without weariness." They "walk without fainting." It all adds up to "joy unspeakable and full of glory." Their cup runs over. Their years never age. They have perpetual youth. "They shall hunger no more, neither thirst any more." God has "wiped away all tears from their eyes"—never again any pain, any fear, any doubt, any defeat, any regret, any stain, any misunderstanding, any sorrow, any temptation, any cloud! What blessedness indeed! What utter joy!

And so we might go on: but continuation would be superfluous inasmuch as no words, however vivid, could communicate that which at present is incommunicable to minds limited by sense and time. How can human imagination tread to within "a stone's throw" of that supernal gloryland? We can but pray the Holy Spirit to make it as real to our present powers of apprehension as will lift us away from worldliness and give us sanctifying longings for that heavenly destiny.

> *How oft on earth the spirit faints,*
> *And mourns o'er inward sin!*
> *But yonder the enraptured saints*
> *Have sinless bliss within!*
> *Oh, for a deeper faith and prayer!*
> *Stir us, dear Lord divine;*
> *Seal us and guard us till we share*
> *That bliss with Thee and Thine.*

J. S. B.

POSTSCRIPT: REVIEW AND PROSPECT

These studies have run away with more pages than I intended. Even so, they have left much unsaid. All I now add is a short review and a parting reflection. As we have noted, belief in life after death is practically universal from earliest times until today; but for authentic revelation on that subject the Bible, the inspired Word of God, is our only safe guide. Its teachings about the Beyond may be summarized as follows.

1. At the death of the body, Christian believers are at once "present with the Lord" in the "third heaven," synonymously called "paradise."

2. All others pass disembodied into sheol-hades until the judgment of the human race at the Great White Throne.

3. At that judgment all will be judged individually. Verdicts will be given, sentences passed, and eternal destinies settled.

4. After our Lord's return to earth in governmental splendor he will set up his millennial kingdom here. His resurrected people will share actively in it as administrators of the Crown.

5. After the Millennium and the general judgment there will be a dissolution of the present cosmic order, and in

place of it a "new heaven and a new earth wherein dwelleth righteousness." The queen city of the new earth will be the "New Jerusalem" in which all the saints of all the centuries will have part, and into which "nothing that defileth shall ever enter."

6. The clear testimony of Scripture is that all who die in babyhood or infancy are saved through the atonement of Christ, and that in the Beyond they develop to full human maturity in perfection.

7. The Bullinger theory of soul-sleep between death of the body and the yet-future resurrection is unscriptural and therefore wrong. The Seventh-Day Adventist teaching of an intervening cessation of personal being is even more astray. The Roman Catholic fiction of purgatory is worst of all, having no biblical warrant whatever, yet so speciously propagated that it has brought, and still brings, millions of people into pitiful delusion and mental suffering.

Finally, I come back to this. No subject can be of more solemn concern to us human beings than that of these studies, namely, *the other side of death*. Dear reader, have you chanced to read the foregoing pages and yet do not know the Lord Jesus as your Savior? If so, let me earnestly entreat you to receive him now.

Reflect: The one and only thing which is certain about your future is that you will die and then pass into that never-ending Beyond where you must stand before the judgment throne of God. Are you ready? Let me urge you: respond to the glad invitation and guarantee of the Gospel. It says, "Believe on the Lord Jesus Christ, and thou shalt be saved" (Acts 16:31).

Turn your eyes and ears to the one-and-only but all-sufficient Savior, Jesus, as on the Cross he makes full atonement for human sin, and as he rises from the grave, the conqueror of death, and as he gives this parting promise in the last book of the Bible: "Behold, I stand at the door, and knock. If any man hear my voice, and open the door,

I will come in to him, and will sup with him, and he with me. To him that overcometh will I grant to sit with me in my throne, even as I also overcame and am set down with my Father in his throne" (Rev. 3:20–21).

As for those of us who know and love and possess him, let us more than ever make him the dearest treasure of our hearts. May we heed Paul's recommendation: "If ye then were raised with Christ . . . set your mind on things above, not on things on the earth; for ye died, and your life is hid with Christ in God." Let us pray daily for his return, and long for the day of days when we shall see him face to face who is the "fairest among ten thousand" and the "altogether lovely."

SUPPLEMENTARY
SKETCH
NONBIBLICAL IDEAS
OF LIFE AFTER DEATH

We sing a hope supreme,
  Outlasting death and time;
Its never-ending vistas gleam
  With prospects all-sublime:
A heaven of perfect love
  Is ours thro' saving grace,
We yet shall drink of joys above
  Before our Savior's face.

Our risen Lord is there,
  Amid those mansions bright,
He said he would our place prepare
  In that fair land of light:
When beats no more the heart
  And these frail bodies die,
In sweet release we then depart
  To dwell with him on high.

What mind on earth can soar
  To where such joys elate?
To see our Lord we long the more,
  And for his coming wait:
Our Lord shall reappear,
  And sleeping ones arise,
And we who then are waiting here
  Shall join them in the skies!

Our Lord's millenial reign
  On earth we then shall share;
As King of all, the Lamb once slain
  Shall bless men everywhere:
Then on, beyond all thought,
  Through ages, perfect bliss!
Oh, may we count the "world" as nought
  For such a hope as this!

In case it may be of interest to some readers, I here give a sketch of after-death concepts outside the Bible. Much fuller treatment can be found in such works as the late Professor S. D. F. Salmond's comprehensive volume *The Christian Doctrine of Immortality*. The following sketch may serve, perhaps, as a useful abbreviation of the varied and plentiful material.

Wide and intensive investigation indicates that belief in an afterlife has existed more or less definitely, in one form or another, among all known races, from the beginning of human history. The differing ideas of it have been considerably affected by geographical and climatic circumstances of different peoples, and by their degree of civilization. The Baperi of South Africa thought that after death souls went to a huge cavern, "Marimatle." New Zealand's Maori tribespeople imagined the place to be at the bottom of a big precipice. Australia's aborigines pictured it as a distant island beyond the western horizon. To the early Finns it was an island called "Tuoni" in the faraway east. Among Mexicans, Peruvians, Polynesians, both sun and moon were thought to be the final place of the departed. Chiefs of the Friendly Islands supposed that after death souls were

237

canoed to a far-off land named "Doobludha."

Arabs of pre-Muhammadan times had an earthy idea of the Beyond. When an Arab died, his best camel was fastened beside his grave and left to die there, so that its master might be supplied with his accustomed mount in the after-realm. But the commonest concept of all seems to have been that the place beyond is a *subterranean* region. The grave itself, deep in the earth, would foster that idea as men peered down into it. Almost everywhere that assumption took hold—among the early peoples of North and South America, the South Sea Islanders, the Zulus and other tribes of Africa, Asiatics, Egyptians, Babylonians, Greeks, and Romans.

In some cases such belief has been infantile and vague; in others more intelligent and organized. It has corresponded roughly with culture level. Among some races it had little or no connection with the way people had lived on earth, whether well or badly. In other cultures it was definitely a place of reward for the moral and of retribution for the impious. Any such view of the future life as one of rewards and punishments has been truer or falser according to a peoples' concept of God, or their worship of fictitious deities.

ASSYRIANS AND BABYLONIANS

The ancient Assyrians and Babylonians who figure conspicuously in the Old Testament Scriptures were the greatest empire-builders of antiquity. The Assyrians were a cruel people to those whom they conquered; yet both they, and the Babylonians, were a religious and literary people, as the many cuneiform inscriptions testify. Outstanding in a literary sense was Assurbanipal, fourth king in the Sargon dynasty, who gathered a great library at Nineveh. The Babylonians, too, have left numerous writings, notably those of the far-famed Nebuchadnezzar. Among a variety of gods, the chief one of the Assyrians was Assur, while the Babylonians came to reverence Merodach as their god-over-all-others.

Evidence of their keen religious disposition is seen in their odes or psalms written a thousand years before Israel's royal David strummed his harp. The spiritual insight of those early lyrics, however, gradually became lost in the agglomerate superstitions of later mythology. As for their concept of an afterlife, there is not the clarity which we find, for instance, in ancient Egyptian religion. They at least believed in an abode of the dead—"Arulu"—a house or land ruled over by a god-king and enringed by the river of death, "Datilla." They also pictured an underworld of demons, the most awesome of which were the seven spirits of the abyss, the so-called Anunaki. The Babylonian mind rose little above those gloomy guesses, though in the epic of Gilgamesh there are references to a resting place of heroes, and suggestions of a tree of life. Many more details might be given, but not adding much further enlightenment.

ANCIENT PERSIA

Beyond Babylon's capital on the Euphrates and Assyria's Nineveh on the Tigris, were a great people of long ago: the Medes and the Persians who later blended in a far-sweeping empire which displaced that of affluent Babylon and reached from the Mediterranean right over to the border of India. Their long and changeful history stretches from the ninth century B.C. to the seventh A.D. It reappears and continues today in Iran. Even from earliest times the thoroughbred Persians preferred to be called Iranians. What we know about ancient Persian religion comes mainly from the Zend-Avesta which later (particularly among the Parsees) became the holy book, the sole rule of faith and practice. Parts of it are attributed to Zoroaster.

The early religion of the Persians was too complex for analysis here, but in it we find a clear concept of life after death. There were two main divinities, the one good

(Ahura-Mazda) the other evil (Angro-Mainyush). Persian burial procedures certainly were strange. The corpse of a deceased person was laid naked on some hilltop and raised above ground on a stone slab. When the body was thus exposed, to be eaten by beast or bird, the soul crossed the "bridge of the gatherer." For three days good spirits contended with evil spirits for the soul. Three kinds of destiny awaited a man. If his good deeds were preponderate, he passed to the Garo-damana, the song-filled abode of Ahura-Mazda. If his evil outweighed his merit, he sank into Duzakh, the abyss of foul demons, to suffer the penalties.

WHAT ABOUT INDIA?

What about India, ancient cradle of religious systems embracing countless millions? Peer away back into the misty past as far as investigation can take you, and you will find an original belief in life after death. The Rig-Veda, oldest of all the Vedas, takes us back ten to fifteen centuries B.C., and makes clear that even then primitive Hinduism talked of that after-world. We cannot be sure whether it supposed that continuation of life was to be endless, or otherwise, but the belief was there, along with an apparent distinction between good and bad people in the Beyond. Only later, by gradual stages, did it become speculative and develop into pantheism with its abstract philosophies of the Beyond—transmigration and ultimate extinction of personality. No, in its infancy Hinduism seems to have taught a bright realm of happiness among the gods for the good, and a nethermost darkness for the bad.

Even Buddhism, despite its break from Hinduism, and its passion for oblivion, had its doctrine of reward and retribution, its twenty-four heavens on the heights of "Maha Meru," and its hells of horror beneath the earth, where its inmates had to endure the pain of one who is "struck with iron rods, fed with food like a hot ball of iron, thrown into a blazing pyre, killed with iron hammers, cast into dense darkness, boiled in iron pots," etc. The most stable doctrine of Buddhism is *Karma,* the inexorable law of moral retribution by which "each individual in the endless chain of life inherits all of good or evil from all one's predecessors" and moves on through this present incarnation to further reincarnations after death, either better or worse. The pathetic hope is that eventually, through the endless operation of Karma, one may reach "Nirvana"—passionless peace by extinction of personal life.

To summarize, let me quote from Dr. S. D. F. Salmond's *Christian Doctrine of Immortality*. "This, then is the conclusion of Indian thought. Death is not man's end. He has a future, but of how dread an aspect! The early faith in an immortality with the gods, in which the individual continues to exist, disappears. For the mass of men the future is one in which the soul passes from shape to shape, wears out body after body, and works out its retribution in a hopeless struggle with its demerit, in a perpetual effort to burst the mesh of existence. For the select few it is a future which means, with the Buddhist, the extinction of individuality in Nirvana; and, with the Brahmin, the absorption of the individual soul in the Universal Soul."

THE ANCIENT EGYPTIANS

When we pass from the Ganges to the Nile and explore *Egyptian* beliefs, we are struck again with the antiquity of the belief in human continuity beyond death. Egyptian civilization reaches back more than 3,500 years B.C. The further we go back, the clearer is the evidence of an original *monotheism,* a belief in one God-over-all, and in the immortality of the human soul. Gradually that monotheism deteriorated into polytheism, as is confirmed by the biblical account of Israel's exodus from Egypt. Many writings, dusty with great age, have survived to give us information on the religious distinctives of that long-enduring nation away back in its mighty past. By far the most important is the famous *Book of the Dead,* which preserves quotations from papyrus rolls found in tombs, and from inscriptions on statues or sarcophagi. A remarkable feature is the idea of a judgment for all men after death. The outstanding practice of the Egyptians to offer oblations on behalf of the departed is in itself a testimony to their conviction as to postmortem continuance.

It is impossible to describe in a few words what the Egyptian ideas of rewards and punishments were in that after-existence; there is such variation in successive periods. Those who, by "gift of knowledge" and observing prescribed religious rites, became united with Osiris and other deities went to a blessed hereafter, feasting at the table of Osiris in Ristat, passing into Elysian fields of Aaru where the corn grows seven feet high. Indeed, with a more-than-human life, they could assume such forms as turtledove, serpent, phoenix, crocodile, golden hawk, heron, lotus flower, and more. On the other hand, the destiny of the condemned was believed to be awful: a hell with many compartments, beds of torment, the food of filth, the "devourer" of the underworld, a death never-ending, or distant extermination.

A notable feature in early Egyptian ideas of an afterlife is the emphasis on *bodily* continuance. The idea of a completely disembodied existence was foreign to them. The life after this was somehow more or less material. That is why the Egyptians did so much embalming of bodies and built such time-enduring pyramids for them. It used to be thought that at one time the Egyptians believed in metempsychosis—a form of transmigration; but that seems now to be disproved. What we stress here is the fact and form of their belief in life after death.

GREEKS AND ROMANS

Who has not heard of those fantastic Greek gods and goddesses of Mount Olympus, and the balcony of deities, higher and lower, male and female, in the Roman Pantheon? Those early Greeks left their impression on the world of thought more than did any other people. It has been rightly averred that "in their reasonings we see the highest achievement of ancient speculation concerning the soul and its immortality." As for the early and later Romans, builders of the most famous state of ancient times, originally owning one small city but subsequently an empire covering a large part of Europe, northern Africa, western Asia, from the Atlantic to the Euphrates, what a legacy *they* have left us through their governmental and administrative genius! What then, of those two great peoples as to their religions and their ideas about the other side of death?

With the *Greeks,* or Hellenes, we have a starting-point away back in the ninth century B.C., the time of Homer. At that period, the gods believed in were not mere shadowy nature-powers, as later, but personal beings; and ideas of the Beyond were simplex rather than complex. By and by those ideas developed into the highly imaginative and artistic. Yet as Fairbairn says in his *Studies in the Philosophy and History of Religion,* "No ancient people seemed so little conscious of any religious connection" between this present life and that which lies beyond.

Away back in the Homeric age, life here in the body was the *real* life—an idea which long persisted. As Dr. Salmond says, the "throbbing, tangible existence that now is, with its familiar activities, its domestic charities, its substantial joys, the glory of arms, the affairs of soldiery, the engagements of hospitality, makes *life* in all its strength and fulness; and [for the Greeks] this bright world of sense is the theatre of man's real being." Therefore death was the sorest of all ills. Whatever may survive death, it is not the full man.

What, then, survived after the dreaded dissolution called death? It was the "soul," though not in *our* sense of the word, but a ghostly form; not the real person, but only an attenuated semblance. There was, however, a real *place* to which all went, good and bad alike; a place named after its grim, dark king, Hades (later Pluto). All the departed must go to the halls of Hades, in which unseen realm, along with Pluto, was a dread queen, Persephone. That desolate domain was a horror even to the gods. The clang of the departed was as "the noise of vultures or the gibbering of bats." Everlasting night enswathed it all. There were rivers of hate and fire. Those and other peculiarities belonged to that dreary after-land from which there was no known extrication.

Later came the famed Greek philosophers, most notably Socrates, Plato, and Aristotle (470–322 B.C.). With them superstition gave place to speculation. In Socrates and Plato there is a groping after the true God; though whether the thinking of the philosophers got down to the mass of the people is very doubtful. So far as an afterlife is concerned, it would rather seem that the "common crowd" rose little above the earlier vagaries.

In Plato, Greek thought on the hereafter reaches its highest and noblest attainment. His doctrine of a future life rests not upon instinct but on *reason.* Furthermore, there is an after-death *judgment* for all souls, based upon their behavior here on earth: a heaven for the pure; a hell for the impure; also a gradation of punishments. As to the *kind* of existence in the Beyond, however, even Plato clings to popular mythical imaginations. Unfortunately, also, he leans on the theory of preexistence, and includes the idea of metempsychosis. Most would agree that his contribution on the persistence of the soul and on the Beyond is the greatest ever built on philosophical speculation: yet at its best, as Dr. Salmond observes, the hope which it offers is "for the philosopher rather than for the man as such."

With Aristotle, Plato's brilliant successor, despite his celebrated argument for the existence of God, there is a flop back so far as human immortality and the Beyond are concerned. He is so indeterminate that some scholars have inferred that he had little or no reasoned belief in either.

Finally, what of the early *Romans?* They gradually became a far stronger people than the Greeks, but the Greeks were *cleverer* than the Romans—cleverer indeed than any other

244

people of the ancient world. All the best books, statues, pictures had come from Greek writers, sculptors, artists. So the Romans not only learned a lot from the Greeks, but also gave up many of their own beliefs. Gradually they came to think less of their own gods and the ideas associated with them. Regrettably, as a result of that, they were neither so simplistic nor so good as formerly. The fascinating Greek gods were baptized into the Roman nomenclature. The Greek supreme divinity, Zeus, became the Roman Jupiter. The Greek Artemis became the Roman Diana. Aphrodite, the Greek goddess of beauty and love, became the Roman Venus; and so on.

Traveling along with that, as the B.C. era drew to its close, big changes in peoples' thinking swept over the Roman world. Epicureanism, Stoicism, and other philosophical systems spread widely, especially among the upper classes. Scipio, Cato, Seneca, Marcus Aurelius, Epictetus, all were Stoics. People of the lower social levels sensed that among the better educated the old religious beliefs were now disdained as juvenile delusions. The historian, Neander, refers to the wide disenchantment with the old religions (among the upper strata) and the revolt against fake miracles and religious deceptions (among the lower levels). The best-educated thought of Rome and its wide-flung provinces seems to have been a mixture of Epicureanism and scepticism with inclination to a pantheistic monotheism. As for the common people, in the rural or "heathen" areas the old religions tenuously held on, but in the populous urban areas their grip had slackened. What else was there to turn to? Along with gross superstition there was a growing incredulity and a widespread pessimism. The words of Psalm 4:6 seem to fit: "There be many that say, Who will show us any good?"

Although the preceding survey has been merely sketchy, certain conclusions may be drawn. Belief in life after death has existed from earliest time among all races in varying forms. Concepts have been vague or sensuous or fanciful, and in some instances ghastly, but the belief itself seems to have been a basic intuition of human nature.

A remarkable feature emerges which all of us moderns should note. The further back we go, the simpler and more like each other the afterlife ideas of the various ethnic groups become; which suggests one common original. Such a common original strikingly accords with the latest findings of archeologists and anthropologists, that the further back we explore, so the clearer do indications become of an original *belief in one God*.

It used to be assumed that monotheism (belief in one God) was a gradual development from a primitive polytheism (belief in a plurality of gods); but now the evidence is the other way round, as Sir Charles Marston has shown in his powerful book *The Bible Comes Alive*. The late Dr. S. H. Langdon, Professor of Assyriology at Oxford, England, wrote in his great work *Semitic Mythology*, "Both in Sumerian and Semitic religions monotheism preceded polytheism." And again, "In my opinion the history of the oldest religion of man is a rapid decline from monotheism to extreme polytheism." Once more in the *Evangelical Quarterly* of April 1937, "It seems to be admitted that the nature-myth gods of India, Greece and Italy, and all Indo-Germanic religions, started with a Sky-God, Zeus, Zeus-pater, Dyauspitar, Jupiter, 'God the father,' all derived from the root *div*, to 'shine,' whence the word *deus*, 'god.' "

As we review the many ideas of life after death, from the misty dawn of the centuries to the end of the B.C. era, do we not see the need for the authentic *revelation* which has been given to us in the Bible? Thank God, we are no longer left guessing and groping. For millions of us the dark mists and gloomy superstitions of human ignorance hitherto are dispersed by the sunrise of authenticated truth. At last we have certainty; for we have the inspired Word of the only true and living God.

To that we may add this. Our deepest instinct seems to

respond to the biblical revelation concerning life after death. There is still much that is *not* revealed, but that which *is* revealed is the most reasonable and convincing to be found anywhere. There is a clarity, coherence, and sanity about it which cannot but appeal to unprejudiced human reflection. Most wonderful of all, to us Christian believers, is the hope which it sets before us—of final deliverance from all effects of sin, of shadowless fellowship with God, and of perfect service for him with our glorious Lord Jesus through all "the ages to come."

Also by J. Sidlow Baxter

Awake, My Heart

With more than one million copies in print, this best-selling devotional continues to challenge and encourage readers with its biblical insight and personal warmth.

"This is a rich mine of information and inspiration."
—*Moody Magazine*

2175-6   376 pp.

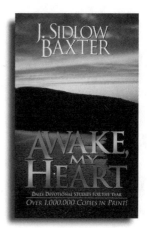

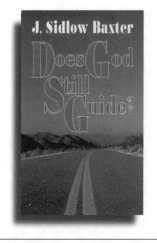

Does God Still Guide?

Baxter offers biblical insights into questions such as, Which is the right way? What's at the end? Is there a sure guide? Does God still guide? and How can I know for certain?

2199-3   192 pp.

Also by J. Sidlow Baxter

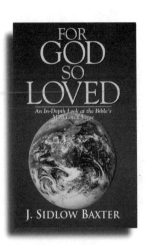

For God So Loved
Baxter examines each of the ten crucial words of John 3:16 as well as the Sonship of Christ, the fate of the lost, and the nature of eternal life.

2173-x   192 pp.

The God You Should Know
Destined to rank among the Christian classics, Baxter shows how ordinary people can come to grips with the extraordinary reality of the Christian life—the God who is here in power, love, and majesty.

2174-8   256 pp.

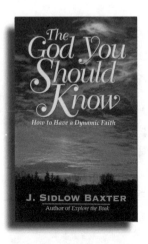

Also by J. Sidlow Baxter

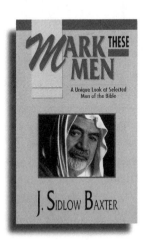

Mark These Men

A treasure-house of Bible biographies including Elisha, Elijah, King Saul, Daniel, Gideon, Balaam, and Nehemiah. Also New Testament characters such as the apostle Paul, Lazarus, the rich young ruler, Ananias, and Simon of Cyrene.

2197-7   192 pp.

The Strategic Grasp of the Bible

An extensive look into the origin, structure, and message of the Word of God. A condensed version of the author's well-known work, *Explore the Book.*

2198-5   406 pp.

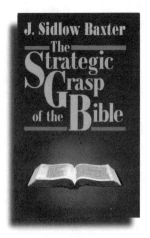

Also by J. Sidlow Baxter

His Deeper Work in Us
Baxter explores the topic of holiness, answering questions such as, Does the Bible teach a deeper, further work of the Holy Spirit in the believer? and Is there a complete freedom from sin?
2172-1   256 pp.

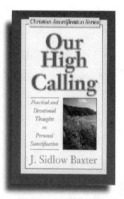

Our High Calling
This volume offers devotional and practical studies to affirm the need for personal sanctification, pointing to the New Testament's emphasis on the call to sanctification as "one of the most ringing of its imperatives."
2171-3   208 pp.

A New Call to Holiness
This volume examines the right approach to Scripture while guarding against the errors that have beguiled others in discussing the question, What is holiness?
2170-5   256 pp.

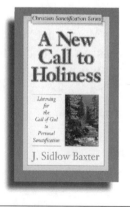

1042